Ni Howdy!

Ni Howdy!

An American Woman's (Mal)Adaptation to Life in the People's Republic of China

Desi Downey

iUniverse, Inc.
New York Lincoln Shanghai

Ni Howdy!
An American Woman's (Mal)Adaptation to Life in the People's Republic of China

iUniverse books may be ordered through booksellers or by contacting:

iUniverse
2021 Pine Lake Road, Suite 100
Lincoln, NE 68512
www.iuniverse.com
1-800-Authors (1-800-288-4677)

This work is based on the author's personal experiences while living and working inside the People's Republic of China; however, some names, events, places and character descriptions have been changed in order to preserve the innocence of the innocent and protect the integrity certain people's privacy.

ISBN-13: 978-0-595-34236-5 (pbk)
ISBN-13: 978-0-595-79008-1 (ebk)
ISBN-10: 0-595-34236-1 (pbk)
ISBN-10: 0-595-79008-9 (ebk)

Printed in the United States of America

For Justin,
who took me there.

The Buddhists say that whatever brings you joy will eventually bring you pain.

I say that if you are very, very lucky—like I was in China—whatever brings you pain may eventually bring you joy.

—Desi

Contents

Foreword
When West Met East: on Desi Downey's "Ni Howdy!"

This is a hilarious personal account of what happened when the West, a/k/a Desi Downey, bumped herself into the East in the early 1990s. At the time, China, with the exception of its few coastal cities, had not been touched by the rampant capitalism of the later days. Big Brother had a monopolistic grip on what it deemed as "suitable" information that its vulnerable populace could be safely exposed to. And no one knew better.

This was the era prior to the explosion of information. There were no bootlegged VCDs of American movies to tell the stories of a different world. The few who ventured out to listen to BBC or Voice of America did so at their own risk. No solace from TV either. Computers were localized and idolized in inland China. Colleges prominently showcased PCs, as symbols of progress and modernity, to visitors. But like the statues of Mao, display of PCs was for awe-inspiring only. They were for the public to view, mostly: keep your dirty hands off (Mao or the computers), mind you. In short, China was a closed society at the time.

It was against such backdrop that our innocent meteorite, Ms. Desi, out of her pickup truck riding, country music-blasting, hee-haw orbit of Nebraska, rammed straight into the mother ship of the quintessential, proletarian China. The rest, as the cliché goes, is history.

With her cunning insights, Desi recounts her daily dilemmas in China, releasing rounds and rounds of unrelenting humor and laughs.

Literally, Desi Downey becomes Lucille Ball, and the setting becomes China Inland. Through her vivid depictions, the passive readers are transformed into active viewers. We, the readers, actually "see" the farces played out from the vision of our mind. We identify with Desi as if we were there. We seem to join in the same adventures, feel the personal perils and stakes on the line, and encounter the universal struggles in coping with the divide of languages, foods, cultures, bureaucracies, and, not the least of all, toiletry.

For those who know Desi personally, she is not unlike Lucille Ball. She exhibits the personal traits that one would easily recognize from Lucy—hastiness, absent-mindedness, poking-curiosity, strong-headed tenacity, and a bit of American centrism. It is an inflammable, dangerous mix in its own right. Put her in China, and the outcome becomes inevitable: she was (and still is) a "bull" in a China store. Or something like that. You know what I mean.

George Wang (A friend who was there)

Introduction

I was a child of the Sixties and I had been taught to believe that all Chinese people were brainless, mindless robots programmed by the evil Red Communists to sustain a deep and burning hatred of every American. My childhood had been filled with all the terrors of that era: the McCarthy witch hunts, the Cold War, the Socialist implications surrounding President Kennedy's assassination, the Cuban Missile Crisis, bomb shelter drills, the Red Scare. "The Commies are coming! The Commies are coming!" was the motto of the day, and too much propaganda on American TV had struck an everlasting fear of the outside world deep into my heart. These beliefs had been so deeply ingrained in my psyche that I didn't even think of the Chinese as people. They were machines, robots. They were evil androids, like the Borg, and their collective Commie consciousness was evil, too.

They were not human and not of my species.

I was a world-class xenophobe.

So, when my husband Justin asked me if I wanted to go live in China for a couple of years while he went off in pursuit of corporate glory as the engineering manager of some obsolete pharmaceutical manufacturing company in Sichuan, I thought he was crazy.

And crazy it was.

But the war was over.

Mao was dead.

And all the Commies were turning into capitalists.

So, in spite of all my racist delusions, by the first of December, 1994—only three short weeks after Justin first asked me if I wanted to go—we went.

Yeah, it was crazy.

Or maybe it was just me that was crazy.

To this day, I still don't know.

❂   ❂   ❂

We stayed in China not for a couple of years, but for four.

And then we left for a year.

And then we went back for two more years.

There were times when I hated it and times when I loved it.

Although at first I had serious reservations about leaving the safe shores of my American homeland for such a reputedly diehard Communist country as China, it turned out not to be a nation filled with over a billion vile, brainwashed, evil androids but regular people, just like me. People who got up every morning and went to work everyday. People who ate, slept, laughed, shit, cried, fucked, had a baby, hid from the government if they wanted to have two, put their pants on one leg at a time, had few qualms about expressing their opinions, and dreamed of a better life, just like me.

Justin and I were welcomed into the homes and the lives of the Chinese people we met with open hearts and open minds; with what I can only describe as down-home American-style country hospitality. It was only natural then, and especially since I'm from Nebraska, that the common Chinese phrase *Ni hao* (pronounced "knee how") evolved, for me, into *Ni Howdy!*, an expression which pretty well just sums up my entire Chinese experience. My three and a half decades of racist delusions disintegrated right before my eyes, and there wasn't a blooming bloody thing I could do about it.

Yes, of course, I still believe wholeheartedly in democracy. I didn't "go Commie." I love my freedom and I would not be separated from my U.S. passport for all the tea in China, so to speak. Uncle Sam is still, and always will be, my hero.

Next to Justin, of course.

But during all the years that Justin and I lived and worked inside the People's Republic of China, I discovered, much to my surprise, that the Chinese are people, too.

Chapter 1
Honey, It Shore Ain't Nebraska!

Maybe I should have listened to that stranger at the airport. Or maybe not.

ο ο ο

Justin and I were waiting for the elevator at LAX, the big international airport in Los Angeles, California. We were on our way to Chengdu, Sichuan, China via Hong Kong. A woman of obviously corporate-clone descent, who was a complete stranger, had been studying us, our cargo (two trolleys crammed with thirteen heavy, overstuffed backpacks and bags), and what must have been my terror-stricken face, for quite some time. As the three of us and all of our luggage squeezed onto the elevator, she continued to review this most bizarre scenario. Finally, she could stand it no more. She leaned in close and whispered politely into my ear, "I don't mean to be nosy, but are you *moving*?"

I nodded, then swallowed hard as I tried to find my voice through my fears. "Yup, to China," was all I managed to squeak out without bursting into tears. Again.

Her eyes grew wide. She shook her head in awe, gazed at me with an infinite amount of sympathy and compassion in her eyes, and gasped. "Oh, my!" she exclaimed. "You must be very brave!"

The elevator doors slid open and she got off, never to be seen or heard from again. Justin pushed his over-burdened trolley out, and then held the doors open for me to disembark with mine, but I was frozen to the spot. There was too much fear. I was so damn scared. I was suffocating and I couldn't breathe. LAX: last stop before the other side of the planet and life as I knew it. I was on the verge of full-blown hysteria, but I knew I had to get a grip. I wanted to go to China, *really*, I did. Honest. But I was a simple Nebraska country girl; literally, fresh off the farm.

I forced myself to breathe. I took a deep breath, or two, or maybe it was three, counted to ten, or maybe it was twenty, and forced my legs to carry me forward, off that airport elevator, and toward my new life in China.

But to this day, that woman's words still haunt me.

Were we truly brave, or *just plain stupid?*

Even after having lived in China for more than six years, I still don't know.

☯   ☯   ☯

We'd been out of America less than a week, and in mainland China for only about six minutes, when I discovered, much to my disgust, that the natural order of things in the East did not quite carry on in the civilized manner to which I had become accustomed to back home in the good old American Midwest.

The past week had been a whirlwind of activity. We had spent God-only-knew how many hours on airplanes and in airports, three awesome, unbelievable days in pre-takeover Hong Kong, and now our plane to Chendgdu, Sichuan, China had just landed.

I was now deep in the heart of communist China.

En route I had convinced myself that an AK47 machine-gun-toting Red Guard welcoming committee would, by simple virtue of our U.S. passports, shoot us down on sight the second we set foot onto the tarmac. That, at least, hadn't happened and I, to put it mildly, was thoroughly relieved. So relieved, in fact, that once we'd cleared Immigration, I immediately went off in search of the bathroom.

I had never seen a Chinese squatty potty before, I'd never even heard of a squatty potty before, not even in Hong Kong, and I was totally unprepared for the sight of that slimy, grimy, dirty, greasy, moldy, gaping black hole pretending to be a toilet staring up at me from the bowels of the dirtiest tile floor in the universe. Yes, one glimpse was all it took, and once I found it, I wished I hadn't. Most definitely, unequivocally, and without any shadow of a single doubt, I did not have to go that bad. And never, ever would. Not so long as I lived. Not even if I was dead.

Just that one quick glance of that god-awful thing convinced me that trying to use a squatty potty would be a hundred times worse than any Red Guard welcoming committee ever could have been, even in my wildest imaginings. And we hadn't even left the airport yet!

It was, up to that point, the most terrifying experience of my life.

I tried not to think about what other possible horrors might lie ahead. Nothing, absolutely nothing, could be worse. Right?

Yeah, right.

I choked. I gagged. I held my nose and ran screaming for the nearest five star hotel and, hopefully, a civilized person's sit-down toilet.

I was in big trouble.

☯   ☯   ☯

Justin and I knew that Sidney, Justin's boss, had dispatched Mr. Wang, company driver, to collect us from Chengdu's Shuangliu airport. We didn't know Mr. Wang and he didn't know us, we didn't speak Chinese and we'd been told he didn't speak English, but new *lao wais* (foreigners) in town were fairly easy to spot, and we knew that Mr. Wang had been ordered to be on the lookout for us.

But Wang hadn't appeared and we, along with what were now fifteen instead of thirteen overstuffed backpacks and bags (our luggage had bred some in Hong Kong), were trapped in Customs. No one there spoke English, either.

I'm sure it was a game to them. They must have been really bored, because they certainly took their own sweet time, and they obviously intended to search through everything—every single backpack, bag, book and magazine. I'd brought a bunch of my favorites along—*Log Home Living, Country Life, Cosmopolitan*—and when they started flipping through the pages and staring at the pictures, I prayed that brassiere ads were not considered pornographic by the Chinese government.

Chinese jail was definitely not at the top of my list of fun places to go. It took a couple of trips in and out of the country before I eventually learned not to look like such a victim every time I crossed the border. Seasoned pros knew that all you had to do was just breeze past these guys and pretend not to notice or understand them. But back then, on that first night, I was scared and stupid and so very naïve, and it was sheer hell.

The Customs search was taking a really long time, and I still hadn't found a decent bathroom. They were x-raying and unpacking and re-packing our luggage and giggling and chattering and pointing at us like we were the week's entertainment (we were). This went on for what seemed like forever. Then, along about the fifth or sixth bag, a four and a half foot tall Chinese tornado rushed into the room and stormed up to the counter. At the top of his lungs he started screaming at the Customs boys going through our stuff. They started screaming back, waving their arms around, still pointing at us and giggling, but the little whirlwind who had just breezed in ignored them. He snatched up two of our smallest bags, beckoned for us to follow suit, and made a mad dash out the door toward the parking lot.

We didn't have a clue as to what was going on, who he was or where he wanted us to go, but we figured nothing could be worse than being stuck in Chinese Customs all night, so we went for it. There were obviously powers-that-be at work here that we just didn't understand. So we took our first (but not our last) giant leap of faith in China and the Chinese, hoisted the rest of our luggage onto our fronts, backs and shoulders as best we could, and raced after our apparent rescuer. I prayed that he was Mr. Wang.

He was.

☯   ☯   ☯

Once on the road to Sidney's house, the trauma of the squatty potty and Customs faded fast. Wang was cruising along in the brand new just-imported-from-America Chevrolet company pickup truck at a comfortable 120 clicks per hour, and I was peering out the window, watching the unreadable neon-bright face of China whiz by through the dusky mist and fog.

We'd barely pulled out of the parking lot at the airport—a major feat in and of itself—when I discovered, much to my dismay, that the Chinese all drove like maniacs. It was *beyond* chaos. They drove anywhere and everywhere they wanted to, they turned anywhere and everywhere they wanted to, they passed anything and everything they wanted to anywhere and everywhere they wanted to, they stopped anywhere and everywhere they wanted to, and they made more noise than I had ever heard in my entire life. They refused to stay in their own lanes, they never turned on their turn signals, they didn't heed oncoming traffic, they jammed on their brakes without warning, and they never stopped for pedestrians or bicycles or oxcarts or anything else crossing the road. They honked just to hear themselves honk. They refused to turn their headlights on, convinced that they would save a liter of gas and, therefore, a few *jiao* (cents), for every 1,200 kilometers (about 745 miles) they drove.

Very conservationist.

Driving in China takes a lot of skill, and riding in a car in China is kind of like riding blindfolded on a roller coaster inside the Twilight Zone. For the first six months I refused to sit anywhere but the middle of the back seat, usually with my eyes squeezed shut tight and my face buried in my hands, too scared to look. Then I started hearing about all the good stuff I was missing—like fifty ducks tied to a bicycle or four live pigs on a motorbike—and got over it.

And they all think they're immortal. Nobody ever pays any attention to anything else on the road. Pedestrians schlep across the streets at will, never stopping to look both ways. The operators of all the cars, trucks, oxcarts, man-carts, putt-putt tractors, vegetable wagons, pedicabs, motorbikes, billion bicycles and the zillion people all think the roads were built just for them. Justin always said it was because of Communism—everybody being equal, everybody had the right to be exactly where everybody else was at any given moment.

I think its population control.

Suddenly, a great big rickety old blue truck came from out of nowhere, bearing down on us, in our lane. The driver flashed his headlights off and on in friendly greeting. Wang grinned, pulled himself up taller in his own driver's seat, flashed the headlights of the brand new just-imported-from-America Chevrolet company pickup truck we were riding in back, and tooted the horn a couple of times in happy hello.

What the hell was this?

Another new game?

Chinese Chicken?

Wasn't dodging the Customs boys enough gaming for one night?

Evidently not, because the big blue truck continued to bear down on us, and Wang continued to not get out of the way.

It seemed great adventure was at hand.

I was beginning to miss the airport.

I buried my face in my hands and screamed at Justin to make Wang slow down, get over, whatever, just get out of the way. Justin screamed back with something like, "Whaddya want me to do about it? I can't speak Chinese, and I ain't driving now, am I?"

True.

Lovely.

I peeked out from between my fingers, didn't like what I saw one bit, and shrieked, terrified again. Wang was heading straight for the big blue truck, laughing, pointing, and just having himself a grand old time. At the last possible second, he jerked out of the way and the big blue truck whizzed safely past. Wang drove on, still grinning, looking happy as could be, and quite pleased with himself, beeping goodbye now instead of happy hello.

Everything was just peachy-keen.

☯   ☯   ☯

There were only one or two other close calls on the road that first night, and we eventually arrived at Sidney's house intact. Even so, I was ready to turn around and go straight back home to Nebraska. After the squatty potty incident, the Customs fiasco and the way Wang and everybody else in China drove, in a mere two hours I'd had just about all I could take. But since I couldn't figure out how to communicate these sentiments to either Wang or the nearest taxi driver, I found myself standing on the front stoop of Justin's boss's house instead.

I'd never met Sidney, but I knew that he'd been born in Sichuan some fifty-odd years earlier and that his family had fled to Taiwan during China's great closure—or rather, what the mainland Chinese still lovingly refer to as Mao Zedong's Great Liberation of 1949. After that, Sidney had gone to America, got educated and made his fortune. He was a self-made millionaire (or billionaire—nobody really knew for sure), which made him the richest human being I had ever met in my entire life. He also turned out to be the most irrational human being I had ever met in my entire life. Although he could be generous to a fault, he had a passion for owning people, and if you worked for him, he owned you—lock, stock and barrel—both personally and professionally. If you went to lunch with him, he told you what to eat. If you went to a banquet with him and his Sichuan government cronies, he not only told you what to eat, he told you what to wear, how to fix your hair, and how to put your makeup on. If you worked for him, or happened to be married to someone who worked for him, he told you where to live and who to live with, a lesson I learned quite well on my first full day of my new life in China. The other lessons took a couple more months.

Sidney met us at the front door that first night, his round Chinese face beaming with pride. His precious American trophies—Justin and me—had finally arrived. We gave him BIG FACE, a very, very important thing in China.

After the *ni haos* and the *nin haos* and a host of other insufferable, unintelligible pleasantries, he ushered us down the corridor of his Chinese European-style villa into a pink-granite living room and introduced us to the entourage of little helpers waiting to study us.

There was the housekeeper, a tiny little slip of a girl who appeared to be all of twelve years old (she was actually eighteen and a distant country cousin of Sidney's whose fondest passion was picking her nose while I was trying to teach her English), the current girlfriend-in-residence (an emaciated woman from Beijing of about twenty who was dressed in a slinky, clingy silver gown, who moved with ghostly grace and who wore more makeup than I'd ever seen on a single human face in my entire life), half a dozen people from a couple of Sidney's Chinese companies, and one or two government officials. We couldn't pronounce any of their names, they couldn't pronounce ours and, of course, none of them spoke English, except for "Hello, how are you?" This phrase proved to be absolutely useless, because if we didn't answer with what they'd learned was the absolute correct response ("I'm fine, thank you, and you?"), they'd get all flustered and giggly, go into immediate *ting bu dong* (I don't understand) mode, and not know what to say next. And even if we gave the proper response ("I'm fine, thank you, and you?"), they'd reply with a simple "Fine, sank you" but, after that, could say nothing else.

It was worse than any Red Guard welcoming committee could have been, even in my wildest imaginings.

The inspection was finally over (them of us), and we all sat down and made ourselves comfortable on Sidney's burgundy leather furniture. Although he had lived in the States for years and years, Sidney also didn't speak very good English. What he spoke instead was very bad Chinglish (Chinese-style English), and he was incapable of speaking in a normal tone of voice. Any time he had anything at all to say, he would puff up his chest and shout, full of himself and with great pride in his ability to control others and their lives. He was not a normal person.

Sidney also liked to be the center of attention, and our arrival had taken the limelight away from him for about three minutes. He pulled himself back to the fore with a statement supposedly directed only at Justin and me, but spoken loudly enough for everyone else in the room to appreciate: "You go your executive penthouse company *condomimium* tomorrow!" he bellowed. "Tonight you sleep my house, be my guest!" It was important for Sidney to let the world know that we were his guests and that he would take very good care of us. It gave him BIG FACE.

By that time, I didn't really give a damn where I spent the night. I was tired, my head was throbbing and a million Chinese people were staring at me and chattering away a million miles a minute in a language that I didn't understand, and I was sure that they were all talking about me. I was hungry, and the Chinese tea Sidney had ordered me to drink was making me sick. I still had to go to the bathroom, but Sidney hadn't yet seen fit to dismiss me long enough to go visit the potty which, thank God, I'd spotted as being the civilized sit-down kind when we'd walked down his front hall.

For that, I was eternally grateful.

Chapter 2
Home-Sweet-Chinese-Home

The following morning I had forgotten all about the traumas of the previous evening, and I woke up ready to explore. My sense of adventure had returned, and I was excited and happy. It was all just sooooo cool.

I hadn't been attacked by any Red Guards, I'd seen no machine guns (except for the ones carried by the security men at the airport in Hong Kong and they didn't count), Wang had rescued us from the clutches of Customs with all our stuff intact, I'd convinced myself that his and everybody else's driving couldn't really have been all that bad, and I'd found a decent bathroom.

Everything was just peachy-keen.

So here I was, inside the People's Republic of China! *China!* Me! I actually lived in the People's Republic of China! Things like this didn't happen to people like me. Driving across the Nebraska/Iowa state line used to be a big deal; now, I was halfway around the planet and living in a foreign country!

It was the opportunity of a lifetime. I would widen my horizons and get the absolute most out of this experience. Yes, indeed-y, I was gonna expose myself to everything. I would get to know the people and learn to understand them. I would talk like they talked, think like they thought, walk like they walked, dress like they dressed, dance to their music, ride a bicycle, devour Sichuan food, drink warm *Tsingtao* beer, smoke their cheap Pagoda cigarettes, learn to sing *kari-yucky* (karaoke), and sleep on a bamboo-grass mat. I couldn't wait to get started.

I got up, took a shower (fortunately the electricity stayed on which meant there was a little hot water), and went downstairs to breakfast. Justin was already at the table. My butt had barely grazed the seat of the empty chair next to Sidney when his little country-cousin-of-a-house-keeper-turned-cook, whose name was Miss Lu, set a bowl of stringy, slimy green goo down in front of me. It appeared to have begun life as a vegetable but recently died a limp and scalding death in a vat of smelly fish oil at the bottom of a wok. On top of the green goo slithered a raw, runny "fried" egg. I despised my eggs that way but it wasn't until the third morning, when Sidney was bragging to me about having told Miss Lu to fix our eggs American-style (which he defined as raw) rather than the Chinese way (hard as a rock), that I managed to convince him that I preferred mine Chinese-style. After that, I usually had at least one thing to eat almost every day. Because, God and Buddha too forgive me, I hate spicy food, I hated the Chinese food in China, I hate Sichuan food, and I hated the food in Chengdu.

Complementing the grand appetizing fare of that first morning's completely unappetizing breakfast was a snot-green plastic colander full of buns-with-meat-in-the-middle (that was great, I'm a vegetarian), no butter, two steaming bowls of Sichuan's favorite spicy red spices (*hua jiao* and *la jiao*—the stuff that makes them famous), the ever-present cold and lumpy white rice and, of course, yellow-green pee-colored tea with leaves and flowers and sticks floating around in it. And no coffee.

It was all really gross, but even this disgusting stuff did nothing to dampen my high spirits on that first morning. I pushed my food around in my bowl with a pair of splintery wooden chopsticks I didn't know how to use and waited for the day's adventures to begin. Sidney jabbered on and on for about forty-five minutes about I had no idea what, constantly waving his *kwai zhi* (chopsticks) around in the air, talking with his mouth full and spitting half-chewed bits of rice and gooey green stuff all over me.

Finally, mid-sentence and mid-flourish, he pushed his bowls aside, and with most of breakfast still lodged in his teeth or dribbling down his chin, announced that it was "time to go visit office and inspect new executive penthouse company *condomimium* now."

Wang, who'd appeared at the front door halfway through breakfast like the good little shadow, company spy and quasi-bodyguard he was, stood at the ready. The brand new just-imported-from-America Chevrolet company pickup truck Wang had retrieved us from the airport in the night before had been retired to parts unknown, and that morning was replaced by a sleek, shining, midnight-black Audi that was the exact same color as his greasy comb-over hair.

We didn't have far to go. The compound that housed the offices and our condo was just around the corner and across the street—about a block and a half away by American standards—but Sidney never walked anywhere, so Wang drove us over there. The offices took up the first two floors of an ugly, soot-covered, pale blue and pee-yellow concrete seven-story building. Our penthouse was five floors above the offices on the top—the seventh—floor. The factory where Justin would spend most of his time was about six kilometers (just under four miles) away, on the edge of the city's limits.

Wang dropped us off in front of our building and went to park the car while Sidney, all puffed up and proud of himself, ushered us into the ground-floor lobby of his company's Chengdu offices. I could feel the excitement in the air. It was obviously a red-letter day. The aliens had arrived. I fully expected a couple of government vans to appear at any moment and the MEN IN BLACK to whisk us off to a secret underground laboratory for further study and evaluation. Everybody—from the cleaning girl to the vice president—was there. Not a soul was working. Fifty pairs of dark, black almond-shaped Chinese eyes were staring at the new white folk.

Yup, it was definitely a red-letter day.

And I felt like a corporate award.

Sidney barked a few Mandarin orders and a short, skinny, olive-drab man with Elvis hair and a horse-y face that was too big for his body moved toward me and thrust out a clammy, trembling hand.

"*Ni hao*," he said, "nice to meet you. My name Daniel."

"*Ni hao*," I replied with what I hoped was a big, friendly smile, speaking the only Chinese phrase I knew. I grasped his limp, bony fingers and rattled his hand up and down. "Daniel, hmmm? Is that your real name?"

A puzzled look crossed his face. He shook his head and scanned the faces of his forty-nine peers for help. "*Ting bu dong! Ting bu dong!*" he mumbled with a frantic shaking of his head. A deep flush had begun to creep along his scrawny neck.

He looked like a scared rabbit with nowhere to run.

I turned to Sidney with a questioning shrug.

"Daniel English no so good!" Sidney roared. "He no understand!"

"Why doesn't he have a Chinese name?" I asked.

"I say everybody in COM-PAN-Y must have American name!" Sidney screamed. "Daniel Chinese name Ding Chao!"

I started to ask why "everybody in company must have American name," but before I could get the words out was distracted by a willowy, black-haired, black-eyed Raven Woman decorated with a clingy, gold-embroidered white silk calf-length dress and matching blood-red lips and fingertips gliding toward me on crimson patent-leather heels. She blessed Justin and me with her coyest smile and a curtsey, then turned the same blood-red shade as her lips and fingertips, ducked her head engagingly, turned to Sidney and chattered something unintelligible into his ear.

"Yes, yes!" he exclaimed. "We go upstair now, see executive penthouse company *condomimium*!" He shoved Justin and me out the door. Daniel Ding Chao, Raven Woman and Wang followed.

Outside the lobby, I looked around expectantly. "Where's the elevator?" I asked with the pure, unadulterated trust of the innocent.

"Chinese *condomimium* no need elevator!" Sidney yelled.

Yeah, right.

Sorry.

I forgot.

No problem. Our executive penthouse company *condomimium* was only on the seventh floor.

I'd just pop up there on my broomstick.

Yeah, right.

But alas, I'd left my broomstick back home on the farm, so we slowly began the long and tedious climb up the dusty concrete stairs to the seventh floor on foot. About halfway up, Sidney stopped us on a landing. Daniel Ding Chao bounded onward up ahead and Raven Woman tottered along behind him on her four-inch stilettos. Wang paused loyally a discreet three steps below, bringing up the rear-guard.

Oozing fatherly wisdom, Sidney put one arm around me, the other around Justin, pulled us in close and whisper-roared, "Daniel your roommate!"

I could feel my eyes grow wide. He couldn't be serious! He'd told Justin before we'd left the States (or so Justin had told me, anyway) that the Daniel we'd be roommates with in Chengdu spoke English. The Daniel I'd heard tell about was supposed to be our very own personal assistant and guide (babysitter). *This* Daniel—Daniel Ding Chao—didn't speak English!

It just couldn't be true.

"*That* Daniel?" I shrieked, pointing toward the Elvis hair half a flight above.

"Sure, sure, same Daniel, you meet him already!" Sidney nodded happily and blessed me with a jolly, breakfast-laden grin. Justin shrugged and gave me an I-dunno-what's-going-on look.

Well, you bloody well better find out what's going on and be quick about it, too, I thought, but there was really nothing either one of us could do right then and there, so we trudged doggedly upward and eventually reached the seventh floor front door of our new executive penthouse company *condomimium*. With a great big proud smile Daniel Ding Chao produced a jagged, four-sided silver key, unlocked the heavy steel front door of my and Justin's new home and swung it open wide.

It was awful. The main room was a square concrete hole with hideous pale chalky-blue walls that were decorated by four urine-yellow-colored doors and one grimy window. An ugly, threadbare, brick-red indoor/outdoor-style carpet covered the living room floor, pieced here and patched there, every frayed and mismatched square curling up at the edges. Black mold crawled along the walls and across the water-stained ceiling toward the one bare 40-watt light bulb in the center of the room under which sat what must have been Sidney's idea of nice furniture: an overstuffed corporate colonial-blue executive pig-leather sofa and two nasty matching chairs.

Six Chinese people, two of them as yet unborn, stood rigid just inside the entrance, four of them staring at me, wide-eyed with wonder.

As Sidney pushed us into the room, I began to get a sneaking suspicion that there was something seriously wrong with this picture. I didn't even care about the ugly blue walls, the hideous carpet or the creepy old mold. What I did care about was *who-the-hell-were-all-these-people* and *what-the-hell-were-they-doing-in-my-apartment*?

I turned to Justin's boss. "Sidney, who are all these people?" I asked, already suspecting an answer that I knew I didn't want to hear.

Before he could reply, a gloating scared-rabbit-turned-proud-rooster Daniel Ding Chao strutted forward and put his hand upon the shoulder of one of the two extremely pregnant women.

"Wife!" boasted the radiant father-to-be, who then moved on to introduce the others. It was evident that he'd been practicing this part of his English for quite some time. "Wife-Mama, wife-brother, wife-brother-wife—she have baby, too!"

I forced a phony-feeling smile across my face, turned again to Justin's boss—the very man who held my very fate in the very palms of his chubby little hands at that very moment—and asked yet another stupid rhetorical question to which I knew would come another happy rhetorical answer that I also did not want to hear: "Sidney, why are all these people in my apartment?"

He showered me with another beaming rice-infested smile, then graced me once more with a confident dip of his infinitely wise head. "Daniel want to live with Daniel-family!" he bawled. "Executive penthouse company *condomimium* big enough! Nobody want be alone! They help you many 'sings!' No problem! No problem!"

I was about to retort with an acid "*Well, I don't want to live with Daniel-family and I don't need their help with many 'sings!'*" when Justin, standing just behind me, squeezed my elbow hard. "I'll take care of this later," he whispered.

You better! I thought as I bit back my caustic and as yet unspoken words and, instead, asked sourly, "Any of 'em speak English, Sidney?"

"Daniel speak a little English! Nobody else need speak English! No problem! No problem! Why you need speak English?"

I was already not too impressed with the "little English" Daniel spoke, but before I had a chance to point this out to Sidney, his mouth was off and running again.

"Your room over there!" He wiggled jovial fingers toward a remote corner. "Bathroom No. 1 over here!" He flailed an arm toward the solid concrete wall on the right, nearly smacking me in the face and breaking my nose. "Other bathroom back there, next to *your* room!" He pivoted back toward the first obsolete corner, arms winging wide. "Kitchen op-poe-sit Bathroom No. 1, over here!" He gave me a fatherly pat on the shoulder, and honored me with yet another glowing, food-y grin.

After the previous night's airport potty scare I was somewhat leery of all Chinese bathrooms, although by comparison that incident was starting to pale. Compared to this, Red Guard welcoming committees and Squatty Potty Hell would be a walk in the park.

But since Justin had said that he would take care of things, I kind of figured that I might just have to live in this seventh-floor hovel after all, even without an elevator (and hopefully without Daniel-family), so I decided to take a look around. And once I did, I wished I hadn't.

I strolled cautiously over to Bathroom No. 2—the one next to "our" room—and peered through the partially open urine-yellow-colored door. A sinister-looking midnight-blue porcelain rectangle—*a squatty potty*—mocked me from a hole in the center of a rust-stained used-to-be-beige tile floor. The chipped and broken bodies of four missing tiles had been tossed off to one side. A rusty old piece of wire, probably an old coat hanger, was twisted around one end of the flexible plastic hose that was attached to the single, rusty, corroded and apparently cold-water-only valve that boldly struck from the center of a mildewed wall. Its other end had been wedged onto a crusty plastic showerhead that resided on the floor in a pool of mucky water next to the squatty potty hole.

Speechless (something that didn't happen to me very often and which Justin insisted never happened to me at all), I turned away and sashayed over to the urine-yellow-colored door of Bathroom No. 1.

And wouldn't you just know it?

Bathroom No. 1 looked exactly like Bathroom No. 2, missing tiles and all, except it didn't have a shower, not even a cold-water-only one.

I backed away from the door of Bathroom No. 1, turned, and headed for the itty-bitty kitchen. The whole damn family, along with Justin, Sidney and Daniel, were still huddled by the front door and gawking at me. Justin looked like he was either afraid to see the apartment for himself or afraid of my potentially violent reactions.

As I moved toward the kitchen, Sidney barked an order in Mandarin, and he and the whole damn family skittered across the living room floor and proceeded to make themselves perfectly comfortable on my new overstuffed corporate colonial-blue executive pig-leather sofa and two nasty matching chairs.

Justin must have thought the kitchen was safer than the bathrooms, because he followed me into that room, and we inspected it together. The concrete counter-tops, concrete shelves and concrete box sink were all covered with four-inch used-to-be-white ceramic bathroom tile squares, inside and out. A corroded steel pipe was connected to a single rusted valve that stuck out of the wall above the tile-covered concrete box sink. I turned it on and frigid water charged out, ricocheted off the bottom and splashed me in the face, then drizzled out a jagged hole chiseled in the bottom toward a drain in the floor two feet below which hadn't seen any Ajax since the dawning of the Cultural Revolution. Justin reached over and turned the water off before I got completely soaked. There was not a hot-water faucet in sight.

Atop a greasy two-burner gas stove sat an ancient wok, still reeking of that morning's rankly arid breakfast. It smelled like somebody had left their tennis shoes in the dryer too long.

Opposite that sat a humming, snot-green, toy refrigerator.

Lovely.

I had to get out of there. Justin followed me back into the living room, where I confronted his boss. "Sidney," I asked, "this place got any hot water?"

Another fatherly grin split Sidney's cheery round features. He gleamed. "You no need hot water!" he bellowed. "Why you need hot water?"

Humbled in light of this supreme bit of wisdom, I hung my head in shame and felt like the epitome of the spoiled, ugly American for even having had the audacity to ask such a silly question.

Justin said it was like going back in time sixty years.

Welcome to China.

Chapter 3
Whatsa *Mai Cai?*

I got my bourgeois way. As determined as I was to fit in, as resolved as I was to get the most out of our Chinese experience, honestly, that was just too much. There was not a snowball's chance in all eighteen levels of hell that I was going to live in an executive penthouse company *con-domimium* with seven-to-be Chinese people and "a little English." I loathed cold showers. Squatty potties were an abomination.

Justin talked to Sidney privately and "Daniel-family" soon moved into new quarters.

Then Justin called a plumber.

We moved into our new Home-Sweet-Chinese-Home a week later. I idolized my sleek new white porcelain gods-with-a-seat. I worshipped my new hot water heater with a vengeance.

Now all I had to do was set up housekeeping. The routine of (or lack of) life in China began.

Every weekday morning Wang collected Justin and drove him off in pursuit of corporate glory (to what I wrongly assumed for months was a fancy air-conditioned office at a fancy state-of-the-art factory out in some high-tech industrial zone), and I was left to fend for myself.

Once we'd moved into our new executive penthouse company *con-domimium* my first order of business was, of course, to find a supermarket and stock the kitchen so, on the morning of the day after moving-in day, as soon as Justin had left for work, I tromped down the seven flights of stairs to the offices in hopes of finding Mr. Elvis Hair, a little English and directions to the nearest grocery store. There was no sign of Daniel

Ding Chao, but Raven Woman, all black and gold silken-clad that day, sparkled out from behind the receptionist's desk. She looked up from the Chinese fashion magazine she was reading as I stormed through the front door of the lobby and, in perfectly pronounced English, asked, "May I help you?"

I was flabbergasted. "I…I…uh…I—*you speak English*?" I stuttered.

She gave me a flawless blood-red-lipped smile. "A little," she answered.

"I…uh, well, yes…, yes, yes, you can help me," I said. "I want to buy groceries. Do you know where the supermarket is?"

Immaculate blood-red fingertips reached into a broken desk drawer and carefully withdrew a worn English-Chinese dictionary. "How to spell?" she asked.

"How to spell what?" I answered.

"How to spell?" she repeated.

"How to spell what?" I asked.

"May I help you?"

"Yes, please, I want to go to the supermarket."

"How to spell?" Raven Woman asked again.

"How to spell what?" I answered again.

Her smile faded. "May I help you?"

"Yes, please, I want to buy groceries."

"You want buy something?"

"Yes, yes! Groceries! I want to buy groceries!" I shouted. Now we were getting somewhere.

She tipped her head. "How to spell?"

"How to spell what?" I asked.

"You want buy something?"

The penny dropped. "Yes, yes!" I cried. "Food, food! I want-buy food!" I had just learned to speak Chinglish.

She nodded. Enlightenment was at hand. "Ah, you must go *mai cai* buy food," she said.

"Whatsa my-tie?" I asked.

That, I never should have asked.

☯   ☯   ☯

Shopping for fruit and vegetables was like foraging through a dark and scary forest.

Shopping for meat was like going on safari.

There were twelve million people in the Chengdu basin and not one single supermarket. At least not one single American-style supermarket. Chengdu, however, just happened to be the home of the largest wet-market—*mai cai*—in all of southwest China.

Lucky me.

Raven Woman, whose real name was actually Miss Li (pronounced "Lee" in Chinese), took me outside and down to the corner and showed me where to go. It turned out that the market was only about a kilometer (maybe half a mile) away, so I set off boldly on my own in search of sustenance.

The *mai cai* was morbid, utter chaos. I wandered alone and forlorn throughout the muddy, bloody, gory bedlam and scanned the hundreds of produce-laden carts and wagons and tarps on the ground, looking for something even remotely familiar to eat. I saw not a single head of recognizable cabbage nor a solitary head of recognizable lettuce. What might have been green beans were three feet long. The freaking carrots were red. I could find not one single box of dehydrated food, not one solitary can of good old open-and-heat Campbell's soup, no pretty little envelopes filled with add-water-boil-and-simmer powdered gravy mix.

How was I supposed to cook?

What were we going to eat?

I wanted to go home.

To Nebraska.

The weird-looking fare of the food stalls lining the streets of the *mai cai* was utterly foreign to me. I felt like I was trapped inside a Salvador Dali Hinky Dinky with no escape.

It was hopeless.

Justin and I were destined to starve.

But, wait! Just what was going on here, anyway? Hadn't I vowed to expose myself to every Chinese thing I possibly could?

Where was my sense of adventure? Back home on the farm?

I took a deep breath, or two, or maybe it was three, counted to ten, or maybe it was twenty, gagged on the rancid fragrance of rotting produce and freshly butchered flesh, and plunged right in.

I shoved my way through the crowd and the chaos of the Chengdu *mai cai* toward a fruit cart filled with little round green things. Somebody shouted, "*Lao wai, lao wai!*" and a group of looky-loos immediately engulfed both me and the filthy wagon and proceeded to engage in the Chinese national pastime: gawking at the foreigner.

I picked up a little round green thing, decided it was a lime, and asked the withered old man behind the cart, "How much is this?"

He answered with a blank look and a stupid grin that showed off the rottenest, blackest teeth I'd ever seen. The crowd broke into an excited, unintelligible chattering that I was convinced was all about me.

Well, that was dumb, I thought. I kept forgetting that I wasn't in English-speaking territory anymore. Then I remembered my Chinglish—maybe he spoke that. I tried again. "Want buy," I said, pointing to the lime. He continued to stare at me like I was a purple-polka-dotted-people-eater.

A young woman from the crowd, blushing furiously and trembling badly, eased herself up next to me, said something to the man in Chinese and then, obviously terrified but evidently not wanting to pass up this great opportunity to practice her English, turned to me. Tentatively, she offered, "One *jin,* sree *kwai.*"

Not understanding, I shook my head. "Whatsa 'jean'?" I asked her. "Whatsa '*kwai*'?"

"Is sree Chinese dollah faw one half-kilo Mandawin Owange," she explained, and then, waving three pink *renminbi* notes in my face for show and tell, asked, "You have some *kwai*?"

At some point during this very enlightening exchange the withered old man behind the wagon must have finally gotten the gist of things because he had now filled a flimsy rice-paper-thin blue plastic bag with little round green things and was flapping it wildly at me with one grubby little hand while holding out the other toward the show-and-tell money.

Wait a minute! *Oranges*? They were *oranges*? What the hell kind of oranges were green? Every mandarin orange I'd ever seen came in a pretty little black can with bright, colorful words on the outside and sweet syrupy stuff on the inside. Good God, weren't oranges supposed to be *orange*?

I was dumbfounded.

"You give man sree *kwai* he give you bag-owange," my self-appointed helper said.

I was too flabbergasted to do anything else, so I did.

The crowd dispersed and the girl vanished. The show, for the moment, was over. Once again I was alone and vulnerable, unprotected and now friendless, too. I contemplated my plight as I trudged on through the masses. I was a useless, spoiled American, and I was in big trouble. My culinary skills were worse than Elly May Clampett's, but it had never been a problem in a civilized country like America where all you had to do was open the can and heat up the contents. Here in China, however, I couldn't even identify, much less buy, common everyday fruit without help.

Yes, I was in big trouble.

And this could really get serious.

Dejected, and with a new crowd in tow now, I wandered aimlessly over to another cart and picked up a brown thing covered with green spots that vaguely resembled a potato. One thing I did know how to do in the kitchen was boil a potato, and this green-spotted brown thing certainly looked like a potato. But I was wary now, since the oranges had looked like limes. I dug a cautious fingernail into a tiny spot on the green-spotted brown thing. It certainly felt like a potato. I sniffed it. It definitely smelled like a potato.

It was then that I had one of my infrequent, brilliant ideas: I decided to try and buy some.

I searched the crowd for any sign of the young woman who'd helped me before, but she was long gone.

I was on my own.

And getting desperate.

So I decided to go for it.

And it was there, amid the blood and gore and guts and noise and chaos of the Chengdu *mai cai,* that I took my second giant leap of faith in China and the Chinese.

I pointed to a pile of green-spotted brown things and nodded to the grubby stranger behind the cart. I handed over a crumpled wad of pink and green *renminbi* notes and prayed that he understood.

He did.

He took my money, gave me a *lao-wai*-have-big-money leer that showed off a crooked row of teeth even rottener than those of Orange-Lime Man, and filled a flimsy rice-paper-thin blue plastic bag with a bunch of green-spotted brown things. He produced a dirty metal plate, three frayed strings and a numbered stick, and weighed it all. He pulled a couple of *jiao* from the money I'd given him and then, with a courtly bow, regally presented me with a bag of what were presumably potatoes and some change.

WOW.

It was just like McDonald's.

Encouraged by the fact that I'd done all that all by myself, that it hadn't really been all that difficult, and confident that I hadn't been cheated because I'd got some change back, I felt braver now.

But not for long.

I moved away from Mr. Potato Head and the green-spotted brown things in search of something else to eat. I passed broken-down baskets of rice; strange looking piles of dried wild mushrooms; white tofu, brown tofu, yellow tofu and blood-red blood-cake tofu; brown gunny sacks full of green-, red-, blue- and brown-spotted dried beans; and spices and powders and dried leaves and curling bark and who-knew-what else. Hundreds of different kinds of fruits and vegetables and stacks of leathery orange and gray and purple noodle-looking things lined the rickety, makeshift tables. Live fish, toads, snakes, eels, turtles and creatures for which I had no name swam or slithered or crawled or hopped around inside row upon row of the red plastic buckets that lined the curbs of every blood-stained street.

It was all just thoroughly disgusting.

Repulsed by the sights and nauseated by the smells, I tried to breathe shallow as I riveted my eyes downward and fastened my vision onto a section of semi-clean asphalt directly between my feet. I glanced up to get my bearings just in time to not-crash headlong into a freshly skinned goat carcass hanging from a vertical rail attached to a bicycle cart.

Now I may have been fresh off the farm, but I was a millenium-age farm girl. I knew that things like hamburger and pork chops and steak were supposed to come from the refrigerator section of the supermarket, all wrapped up nice and tight on sterile white-foam trays and covered with clear, crisp, clean cellophane. Good God, back home in Nebraska nobody ever *killed* anything for supper!

I had to get out of there. Searching for a route of escape, against my better judgment I looked around. Slabs of dripping blue-tinted flesh swayed from rusty iron hooks. The fetid odor of newly-butchered beef assaulted my nostrils, closing in on me, suffocating me. The definition of "fresh" took on a whole new meaning. There were fish eyes and pig parts and chicken's feet lying all over the place.

If I hadn't already been a vegetarian, I would have become one in China, fast. And although I was, Justin wasn't, but we had a deal: he wouldn't make me eat meat if I didn't make him eat tofu. If I happened to be going to the store and he wanted something simple that wasn't too gross, like a sterile cellophane-wrapped package of hamburger, I had no problem picking it up for him. I'd intended to buy some that day, in fact. Trouble was, there wasn't a single solitary pound of ground beef in sight.

Well, I decided, Justin would just have to safari for his own damn hamburger. I'd had enough. I fled, straight through the heart of Butcher's Heaven (or, as it was in my case, Vegetarian's Hell). I raced toward a busy thoroughfare I could see off in the distance that I prayed was *Ren Min Nan Lu*—the People's Road—the road to freedom and Home-Sweet-Chinese-Home.

Of course, just when I thought things couldn't possibly get any worse, they did.

Two blocks to go and I stumbled into a snow-fence-turned-chicken-pen. A *live* chicken pen, with its 55-gallon drum of scalding hot water and gory chopping block standing bloody vigil next door. The squawking of all that doomed fowl, however, brought me to my senses, and I suddenly remembered that another thing I knew how to do in the kitchen was to almost not-burn an egg.

Chickens and eggs. Hmmm…well, I thought, didn't it just seem natural that the chickens would be near the eggs?

So, in a last-ditch effort to supply poor Justin with something even remotely edible for dinner that night after his hard day at work in pursuit of corporate glory, I looked around the *mai cai* for the egg cartons.

That was dumb.

Eggs don't come in cartons in China.

They do, however, come in raggedy old baskets tended by raggedy old women, and there were a couple of those nearby.

I went for it.

Three minutes and one more leap of faith later, I clutched a flimsy rice-paper-thin blue plastic bag of eight brown calcium-deficient eggs in my quivering right hand and stopped wondering why the ones on the bottom didn't break when sticky yellow goo began to leak out onto my fingers.

But that was it; I'd truly had all I could take. I raced blindly from the largest *mai cai* in southwest China toward *Ren Min Nan Lu* and the sanctuary of my new executive penthouse company *condomimium* like a woman possessed. As God is my witness, I swore that I'd never set foot outside its steel front door again.

My search for all the staples of civilized life—salt, pepper, cereal, Pop-Tarts, coffee, butter, peanut butter, sliced bread, cheese, soda crackers, milk, spaghetti, spaghetti sauce mix, hamburger, Campbell's soup, macaroni and cheese, flour, baking powder, baking soda, toilet paper and light bulbs (along with all the other things I thought I couldn't live without)—had been, for the most part, futile. All that food at the *mai cai*, and I couldn't find us anything decent to eat. I was truly useless, exactly like one of those spoiled foreigners everybody was always complaining about.

I finally made it safely home, fortunately without further incident. I took my three measly purchases into the tiny bathroom-tile kitchen for inspection. I washed the egg slime and chicken shit off the few remaining unbroken eggs and put them in the toy refrigerator, along with the lime-colored oranges. I stuffed a bandanna into the hole at the bottom of the tile-covered concrete-box sink, filled it with water and bleach I'd brought with me from Hong Kong and soaked the green-spotted brown things into a state of antiseptic edibility.

Then I got serious. I made a list of all the fruit and veggies and common stuff I was sure was buyable in Chengdu, if only I could find it. I took the list downstairs to the office and, with the promise of free English lessons, bribed Miss Li and her bilingual dictionary into translating it into Chinese for me. She even added the average local prices of each item to help keep me from being cheated.

After that, I trudged back up the seven flights of stairs to our executive penthouse company *condomimium*, where I spent the next two hours teaching myself how to count from one to twenty in Chinese so that I could argue with the peasants at the *mai cai* whenever they tried to rip me off.

I was ready.

The next time I went to the bloody *mai cai*, by God, I would go prepared.

Chapter 4
Ma Bell Never Lived in China

I needed to call the American Consulate. I wanted to know what to do in case of an emergency, like if I fell off my bicycle or there was a military coup or something.

I went downstairs to the office one morning in search of the telephone book.

"Miss Li, can I see the telephone book, please?" I asked. Good God, I was *so* very naïve.

Miss Li smiled demurely from above the folds of that day's bright red embroidered silk gown and produced her worn English-Chinese dictionary from her broken desk drawer.

I waved the book away. "No, you no need that, I want-use *telephone* book," I said, speaking Chinglish, which, I had learned, usually worked better than regular English.

"You want telephone somebody?" the sweet Miss Li inquired.

"Yes, please, I want-call American Consulate," I answered.

"You have telephone number?"

"No, I no have telephone number, that's why I need-use telephone book," I explained.

"How you can telephone somebody you no have telephone number?" she asked sweetly.

"I want-use telephone book, look up telephone number, call American Consulate," I said.

"You cannot telephone somebody you no have telephone number." Miss Li stated this fact plainly, as if I was a stupid foreigner.

I sighed. Chinglish was just too much work, so I abandoned it and, in frustrated regular English, said, "Yes, I know that. That's why I want to look up the telephone number in the telephone book."

Miss Li mumbled "*mei you*" and turned her attention back to her magazine.

"Mei you?"

"*Mei you.*"

"What is '*mei you*'?" I asked.

"No have," she stated with finality.

Ahhhh. No have. I wondered if that meant *mei-you*-no-have-telephone-book, *mei-you*-no-have-telephone-number, or *mei-you*-no-have-desire-to-be-bothered-with-you-dumb-demanding-*lao-wai*-any more.

"How can I get the telephone number?" I persisted.

She shook her head and muttered into the pages of Chinese haute couture. "I don't know, *bu zhi dao*," she said. Obviously her fascination with the Great White Goddess turned Great White Pain in the Ass was fading fast.

I resorted to Chinglish again, because she was usually more receptive to that. "Can telephone Information, yes?" I suggested helpfully, pointing to the telephone on her desk.

She tore herself away from her magazine and gave me her full attention once more. "You want some *informations*?" she asked.

"Yes, I want-telephone Information, ask somebody for some *informations*, yes," I told her.

"You want telephone somebody, ask for some *informations*?"

I sighed. "Yes, please, I want to telephone Information and ask for some *informations*," I repeated.

"You have telephone number?" she asked.

"No, I no have telephone number for Information," I said. "You have?"

"No."

"Can telephone Operator and ask for telephone number of Information, yes?" I suggested helpfully.

She raised a curious eyebrow. "*Op-ate-ah?*" she asked.

"You know, dial 'O' for Operator." I jiggled up and down for effect, but she didn't get it. I shrugged. "American proverb," I muttered.

Miss Li opened her dictionary. "How to spell?" she asked.

"O-P-E-R-A-T-O-R."

She flipped some pages. "O...?"

"Yes, O first, then P." I barely managed to keep the exasperation out of my voice. It wasn't her fault that I couldn't speak Chinese, and I had no right to expect her to speak English. It was her country, after all. Still, this was really getting tedious.

"P...?" she asked, running an immaculate blood-red fingertip slowly down the page of her English-Chinese dictionary.

"P, then E."

"E...?"

"E, then R."

"R...?"

"R! R! R!" I screamed. "Then A! T! O! R! Operator, Operator! You can telephone the Operator to get the telephone number for Information so that you can call Information and get the telephone number for the American Consulate!" I snatched the receiver off the phone on her desk and punched the zero with a vengeance.

Nothing. Absolutely no response at all from the other end of the wire. No sweetly familiar busy-buzzing, no ringy, ringy, ring-a-ding-ling. Just total, complete, dead silence. I clicked the little clicky thing in the cradle and listened carefully; there was a dial tone. It sounded just like an American dial tone. Well, this is progress, at least, I thought. I punched the zero again. And got dead silence again. As usual, I was getting nowhere fast.

Good God, I thought, I would have to call 202-555-1212 all the way over in good ol' Washington, D.C. just to get the freaking telephone number of the freaking U.S. State Department just so that I could call them and ask them for the freaking telephone number of the freaking American Consulate in Chengdu, Sichuan, China. (Which, incidentally, once finally found, turned out to be only about six blocks away.)

Miss Li closed her tattered English-Chinese dictionary and turned her raven midnight eyes up toward the wild blue yonder of those of the crazed *lao wai* who stood convulsing above her desk, trying to ring the life out of, or rather into, an innocent telephone machine. She blinked at me once, tired of the game. "Chengdu no have *op-ate-ah*," she said. "*Mei you.*"

I slammed the receiver down and stormed out of the office. I'd seen a telephone book somewhere, probably at Sidney's house, and come hell or high water, I would bloody well find it. I marched across the street and around the corner and rang the doorbell of Sidney's Chinese European-style villa. He wasn't there but his housekeeper was, and she let me in, then scuttled off to hide in her kitchen when she saw what must surely have been the frenzied maniac gleam in my eyes.

I ravaged Sidney's living room until I found it. I tore it open with a fury, and it was only then that I realized that I couldn't read the damn thing. It was in Chinese, of course.

Duh.

No problem. I raced back around the corner and across the street to the office, bolted through the front door of the lobby, and slammed the heavy Chinese telephone book I'd found at Sidney's triumphantly down on top of Miss Li's desk with a loud bang, obliterating the latest issue of Chinese *Cosmo*.

"Telephone book!" I shrieked.

Miss Li was unflappable. She looked up, batted her sparkly eyelids at me, gave me that sweet, demure, coy smile of hers, and MOCKED me. "Telephone book," she repeated, calmly.

"Can telephone American Consulate now, yes?" I asked, hopefully.

"You have telephone number?" she asked.

"No, no, no! I no have telephone number!" I shouted wildly. "But I have telephone book! But I cannot read Chinese telephone book! Please, please, you can help me, yes, please? You can look up telephone number for American Consulate in Chinese telephone book for me, yes? *Please?*" I was begging now.

Miss Li gave me her most innocent stare as she pursed her perfectly-painted blood-red lips and sadly shook her perfectly-porcelain doll-like head. With immaculate blood-red fingertips, she gently lifted the Chinese telephone book from off the top of her desk like it was an evil dirty thing she'd rather not touch and handed it back to me with her answer: "Oh, sowwy, Chinese telephone book *vewy* difficult to use."

Like that counts.

Yeah, right.

I give up.

Chapter 5
Public Enemy Number One

I am convinced that the invention of the squatty potty was a Communist Plot intended to overthrow the civilized Western world.

Ever since my close encounter with the squatty potty at the airport that first night, I had been avoiding them like the Black Plague. But these slimy, grimy, dirty, greasy, moldy, gaping black holes in the floor were inescapable and, even if you could avoid the sight of them, it was impossible to avoid the smell. They reeked.

Squatty potties are an abomination. I decided early on that experiencing the real China did not include crossing over into the squatty potty zone, and I had devised a foolproof plan for avoiding them at all costs. I knew the strategic location of every self-proclaimed three, four and five star hotel lobby-bathroom sit-down toilet in the city, and if I couldn't find one, I went home.

Asians in general, the Chinese in particular and, once in a while even a few *lao wais*, were always telling me how much more sanitary squatty potties were than sit-downs. This, as far as I was concerned, was ludicrous, and I got real sick and tired of hearing about it all the time. Personally, I would much rather park my butt where somebody else's butt has been than try to do a balancing act in a puddle of somebody else's pee while squatting over a dirty hole in the floor while trying to keep my pants legs dry any day.

For the first year or so that we lived in China I adamantly refused to enter the squatty potty zone, although secretly I feared that someday, despite my resolve and God forbid, I might just have to use one. For this reason I actually found myself, and rather sadistically so, fascinated with the logistics of squatty pottying, although I don't think I ever really did figure out how to use one properly.

But for all its primitiveness, the art of squatty pottying was really rather complex. First and foremost, it was quite apparent that proper squatty potty position would require strong thighs, good balance and a wide-angle spread, but the floors around these holes in the floor were always so slippery and wet that it seemed impossible to stay in one place for very long. And then there was that fear of falling in.

Now the Chinese don't have any logistical problems with squatty pottying because they start squatting as soon as they're born. They don't even wear diapers! They wear these funny little crotchless pants that let the family jewels hang free for easy access, and they squat anywhere and anytime they want. Absolutely no place is sacred. Not sidewalks, not streets, not the floors of department stores. When nature calls, the children go, so by the time they're all grown up the Chinese have had plenty of time to build up the muscles in their thighs. I, however, hadn't endured a lifetime of squatty practice, and my spoiled American thighs were lazy and weak and I knew for sure would no doubt constantly be letting me down.

On top of that, I could never quite figure out how to keep the legs of my pulled-down pants germ-free and dry. If my jeans rubbed up against that floor, I thought, they might touch a puddle of everybody else's pee (or something equally as gross), and then, when I pulled my pants back up again, I might get some of that gooey, gunky, awful, slimy stuff on me.

Bluhuck.

Yeeuck.

Barf.

Gross.

And on top of that, there was never any toilet paper in a squatty potty, unless you counted the pile of used stuff in the back corner, and I was always forgetting to bring my own along.

I vowed that under no circumstances whatsoever would I enter the squatty potty zone.

NOT EVER.

NOT NEVER.

ABSOLUTELY, POSITIVELY NOT.

NO WAY.

NEVER, NEVER, NEVER, NOT EVER.

NO WAY.

So I was a spoiled, ugly American.

So what.

So the road to hell is paved with good intentions.

So what.

It was, of course, inevitable. Anybody who spends any time at all in China (or any part of Asia, for that matter), sooner or later, ends up going to THE ZONE. And, as luck would have it, the day I had to go so bad that I just had to enter THE ZONE just happened to be on a day when we were three hours from nowhere, cruising around in the countryside. Trust me, there ain't no five star hotels out in the Chinese boonies, and there ain't no three or four stars either, and it was just too far to run home quick.

It was time for me to confront my deepest, darkest fear. *I* was going to THE ZONE.

I looked around for a tree (I'd take a tree over a squatty any day), but it was obvious that Mao and his Great Leap Forward had been there first, because there wasn't a tree in sight.

Oh, well, I thought. Other people did it. And lived. How bad could it be?

It was bad.

No, actually it was worse.

In my very bad Chinese, I conveyed my need to Wang (*"summa di fan, WC?"*), and we stopped in a small village so that I could take care of things. But the peasants there had obviously never seen a foreigner before—particularly a blonde-haired, blue-eyed, white woman, and when I climbed out of the brand new just-imported-from-America

Chevrolet company pickup truck that Wang had been driving us around in, I instantly became the entertainment of the year.

Foreigners lose all rights to personal space and privacy upon crossing the Chinese border, and if you're from outta town, count on it, the Chinese are gonna stare at you. And, if they hate you because you are an evil imperial capitalist individualist from America, they will not only stare at you, they will spit at you and call you names like "dirty white ghost" and "foreign devil." But, if they love you because you are an evil imperial capitalist individualist from America, they will stare at you, scream *"Hullo!"* at you until they get your undivided attention, and then drive you crazy trying to practice their English and calling you names like "my foreign friend."

By the time I had crossed a couple of rice paddies and reached the raggedy old tarp-covered doorway of the squatty potty shack that day, about fifteen Chinese peasants were following me. Crossing the semi-wide open spaces of the rice fields, this hadn't bothered me a whole lot, because I'd been in China for a while by then, and I'd kind of gotten used to being treated like an animal in a zoo. But by the time I finally reached the tiny squatty shack the whole damn village was in tow. And followed me inside. Men, women and children, old, young and middle-aged, they *all* followed me into the squatty potty shack! Every last one of them.

And squatty potty stalls have no doors.

Lovely.

So many villagers had crammed themselves into the room, in fact, that they were spilling out the tarp-covered entrance. They were pushing and shoving and craning their squinty little necks around, trying to get the best view of the Great White Goddess Come to Take a Village Pee. I wondered if anybody had remembered to bring the popcorn, and I prayed that they wouldn't go prostrate and start bowing and chanting once I got squatted over the squatty-potty throne.

Well, to make a long story short, suffice it to say that I finally got the job done. I'd even remembered to bring my own toilet paper along, but using the communal village squatty potty with a crowd of Chinese peasants looking on was not an experience that rose to the top of my list of fun things to do.

At that moment, on that day in that place, I knew just how the Roswell aliens felt.

Go figure.

☯   ☯   ☯

Despite my public humiliation and my initial troubles with the logistics of squatty pottying, going with an audience actually helped me overcome my phobia, and I was finally free.

Have toilet paper, will travel.

So a few weeks later, on a trip downtown to change some money, when I had to go, I went. I never even gave it a second thought. And I was lucky that day, because nobody followed me. Except that that day, that wasn't really a very lucky thing after all, because I'd forgotten to bring my own toilet paper, and it was one of those very special times when I really needed my own toilet paper.

Bad.

Really, really bad.

So I remained squatted there over the public squatty potty hole for a while, and prayed that somebody would come in (not that I could communicate with them even if they did), but the room remained steadfastly empty. Finally (and a little frantic by now because my weak and spoiled American thighs were definitely letting me down), I began digging through my pockets for a dirty Kleenex or a Harley bandanna or something—anything—that I could use for TP, but there was nothing there. Just some Chinese *yuan*, and the American dollars I'd been planning to exchange.

Wait a minute.

Yuan?

Dollars?

Money?

Paper money?

Well, *what would you do?*

I desecrated the face of Mao and never even stopped to count the fucking zeroes.

It was the American way.

Chapter 6
Hospital Hell

It was early April. I was miserable. It had been a cold and ugly winter, and so far it had also been a cold and ugly spring. Gloomy gray days faded into gloomier gray nights. Lunar New Year a/k/a Chinese New Year a/k/a Chinese Christmas a/k/a Spring Festival had come and gone, and yet the sun refused to show its shining face, and the bone-chilling damp refused to leave Chengdu's noxious purple air. The fog or smog or soot or whatever it was that permeated everything in the city enveloped me, suffocated me, and turned me into a lethargic, non-caring, non-functioning entity. I felt all brown and dry and brittle, just like the dead flowers on the windowsill that I hadn't gotten around to throwing out yet. I kind of liked them there, actually—they were something I could relate to.

The locals swore that spring was just around the corner, and joked that sun in Chengdu was so rare that the dogs barked at it instead of the moon. Sometimes at night I would stand on our balcony and count the stars in the sky. The most I ever saw were fourteen.

Indoor heating was virtually unheard of in Chengdu, mainly, we had been told, because south of the Yellow River it was supposedly illegal. Even so, electric space heaters were popular, but virtually useless, because the power rarely stayed on. Forced-air furnaces didn't exist. The five layers of clothing I was expected to wear to keep warm were intolerable and inhibiting and made me look fat.

I remember thinking when we first got to Chengdu that the Chinese people were not nearly as scrawny as I had expected them to be. Then, when spring finally did come around and they started shedding all those layers of winter clothing, they turned out to be really skinny after all. This also made me look fat.

Despite the crappy winter, Justin and I had looked forward to our first Spring Festival in China. It was the biggest holiday of the year, and we could actually feel the energy and excitement in the air as the Chinese geared up for it. In our rookie ignorance, we had opted to stay in Chengdu for the holiday, anticipating weeks of parades and elaborate floats and colorful Chinese dragons and Mardi Gras-style festivities. Instead, the whole city had shut down like small-town Nebraska after 8:00 p.m. on a weeknight (9:30 on the weekends), and the carnival of joyous, reckless partying and wild, wanton dancing in the streets we expected never came to pass. For that one week, at least, one-point-two-billion Chinese people had forgotten all about babysitting the *lao wais* and opted instead to celebrate their biggest holiday of the year by travelling great distances to hide out with their own families, gorge themselves on Grandma's greasy home-cooking, Grandpa's warm beer, and marathon mahjong games that lasted a minimum of three straight days and nights. For us, Spring Festival was a complete and total bust, and we were bored shitless. Now, at least, we understood why all the other foreigners had bailed out of the country during Chinese Lunar New Year.

The empty promises of Spring Festival having come and gone without the appearance of spring, however, were not entirely to blame for my apathy. I was sick. Very, very sick, and so weak that I could barely get out of bed. For weeks I had stubbornly refused to see a doctor. In Chengdu they stuck an IV in you for everything. If you sneezed, they stuck an IV in you; if you had a headache, a toothache, cramps, a stubbed toe, a broken foot or a broken fingernail, they stuck an IV in you—so I really couldn't see the point. Heaven only knew what was in those bottles and, besides that, I was terrified of dirty needles.

When I got so pale that I looked dead Justin ratted me out to Sidney who, for the second and final time in his life, marched up the seven flights of stairs to our executive penthouse company *condomimium* to see for himself. He took one look at my limp and pallid form and ordered Wang to drive me to the hospital, pronto. I was so weak that poor Justin had to tote me down the stairs on his back like a sack of potatoes.

The hospital where they took me—Chengdu's biggest, best and finest—was indescribable. I don't know if it was the hallucinations of my fevered brain, or my spoiled American expectations, or what, but it was bad beyond words. Primitive. Barbaric. Repulsive. Medieval. My thesaurus suggested I use words like "grossly offensive," "loathsome," "vulgar," "monstrous," "revolting" or "repugnant" to describe it. Not. Even. Close.

The dingy puke-green cement walls were warped and crumbling, the sooty asbestos ceilings were chipped and peeling, the antique x-ray machine (and all the other metal equipment, including anything stainless steel) was rusty and corroded. What I assumed had once been crisp white bed sheets and crisp white nurses had turned a stained and dirty dishwater gray. The windows were grimy, the floors were skuzzy and the corridors were littered with wadded-up tissues, used bandages, blood-stained Q-tips and cigarette butts.

Lovely.

The young Chinese emergency room doctor (who looked to be all of twelve years old but was surely old enough to be a doctor (I hoped)) that I was assigned to didn't speak any English and the nurses didn't speak any English, either, at least not the comprehensible kind. When it was finally my turn, which was actually relatively fast because the Chinese don't like the idea of a sick *lao wai* sitting around in one of their emergency rooms too long, Dr. Twelve took my pulse, showed me how he wanted me to stick out my tongue and then shoved me off to radiology (and I used this term loosely here), where a prehistoric contraption clunked off a few pictures of my wheedling chest. None of my clothing had been removed (even though I was wearing an under-wire bra), none of my jewelry had been removed, and the crowd that had gathered inside the x-ray room with me to engage in the Chinese national pastime (gawking at the foreigner) had not been dispersed. There wasn't a lead blanket in sight. The x-ray machine was so old it looked as if it could only be steam-driven. Each time it went *kerrr-thunkk* I fully expected a puff of smoke to billow from its top.

I felt just like a laboratory rat.

When they finally finished nuking me I staggered back down the hall to Dr. Twelve's public examination room (all examination rooms in all Chinese hospitals are public). "*Deng yi xia,*" he said.

That was a bad sign. *Deng yi xia* could mean anything from a half a second to a half a day in China. But it was better than if he had said *min tian* which, technically speaking, meant "tomorrow," but, in reality, could have meant really big trouble, because "tomorrow" in Chengdu could mean anything from the next day to sometime the following week.

We were lucky that night, though, and didn't have to wait long. About forty-five minutes later Dr. Twelve, after having examined my x-rays under a 40-watt light bulb for about ten seconds, proclaimed proudly in Chinglish that I had "*tub-eee-key-oh-sis*" (tuberculosis) and "must live" in the hospital for one week.

Lovely.

They took me to a private room on the third floor of a wing reserved for Chinese governors and dignitaries and Communist Party leaders and the like. The elevator had been disabled for the night, so Justin packed me up the stairs on his back and deposited me onto the bed in my assigned room. A dingy nurse cranked me into a semi-sitting position, plunged an IV needle into my hand before I could protest and threw a quilt that smelled like urine over me, then left. The weather outside was cold, dark, dank and clammy and the room inside was cold, dark, dank and clammy. There was no heat. Eventually, mercifully, I fell into a restless, chilly slumber.

At 6:00 a.m. the following morning, a plump and curious peasant girl woke me up when she clattered into my room with breakfast: slimy green goo, cold, lumpy rice and warm, leafy greenish-yellow liquid—hospital tea—floating around in a glass. She sat the tray down on my nightstand and skittered from the room, only to return a few minutes later with the filthiest mop in the universe. She swabbed the cold, grimy, gray-aggregate floor with it for about twenty seconds (just long enough to steal one or two covert glances at me from under her shaggy fringe of black bangs) and then scurried out, tittering.

Dr. Twelve appeared about a half an hour later with an entourage of three Chinese nurses and a brand new Chinese-English dictionary. Communication was at hand. He puffed up his chest, flipped open his new dictionary, and offered me a bright, confident smile. "You no have *tub-eee-key-oh-sis*," he announced.

"Lovely," I groaned.

He stubbed his index finger at a word in the dictionary and showed it to me. "You have *puh-nee-moan-eee-ah*," he said brightly.

"Lovely," I groaned. Pneumonia. Well, that was probably better than *tub-eee-key-oh-sis*, anyway. Considering the archaic state of the hospital and the absence of a Chinese-English dictionary the night before, it wasn't any wonder that he hadn't diagnosed me right the first time. I forgave him and assumed that this was good news. "I can go home now, yes?" I asked hopefully.

"You must live hospital one week," he answered.

"Lovely," I moaned.

About that time Nurse Number One got over staring at me and noticed that I hadn't touched my breakfast. "Why you no eat bray-fas?" she asked.

"Make me sick, too sick, no eat," I mourned in Chinglish, but she wasn't buying it. The Chinese hate it when you don't eat what they give you. They will eat anything and everything put in front of them, no matter what, whether they like it or not. Food's food. No doubt this is because they were starving for so long. But a spoiled, wasteful *lao wai* like me takes having enough to eat and what I want to eat for granted. I wouldn't touch the congealed slop on that tray even if they force-fed it to me. I would never be that hungry, not ever. Dr. Twelve and entourage, however, could accept neither my excuses nor my wasteful attitude, and so proceeded to subject me to a banal twenty-minute dissertation that I didn't understand but guessed was no doubt relative to healthy eating and speedy recovery. Last thing they wanted on their hands was a dead white girl, and so, even though the slop on that tray was as likely to kill me as it was to cure me, they wanted me to eat. As they droned on and on I lay there on my cold lumpy hospital bed, tried not to smell the urine-smelling blanket, and studied the flaking asbestos of the ceiling. I wondered how I would get rid of lunch and supper and tomorrow's breakfast and all the rest of the week's hospital food without having to eat it. I wasn't worried about what I would eat, only about what I wouldn't, but it goes without saying that I didn't want to get caught with any more uneaten food left on my tray and be subjected to any more unintelligible lectures. I finally solved the problem by sneaking into the bathroom three times a day and flushing all the disgusting hospital food they brought me down the toilet.

Two days after I was admitted, Justin ended up in the hospital, too. Although it was the first week of April and supposedly spring, winter had been harsh. We just weren't used to Chengdu's muggy, damp, cold, polluted, purple-gray air—a breeding ground for bacteria—and we simply hadn't had enough time to acclimate. Justin was diagnosed with severe bronchitis and a lung infection, and put to bed in a room two doors down the hall from me.

Our hospital rooms weren't really all that bad, if you didn't care about the ugly puke-green walls, the dusty black mold, the peeling, flaking asbestos ceilings and the unfriendly grimy, gray aggregate floors. And the cold. It was *soooooo* cold. But our rooms were large, and our beds were double. We each had a balcony that overlooked a pretty courtyard three stories down, and we each had our own private bathroom complete with cold water sink, sit-down toilet and ancient cast iron bathtub. The tub in my room was so old and corroded that big spots of rust had eaten through the enamel in half a dozen places. About fifty years earlier someone had built a cupboard around the bottom, but by the time I got there, the doors had long since fallen off, and the cavern within appeared to be filled with eons of unspeakable trash. Not that I got down on my hands and knees with a flashlight and looked, now, mind you, but I could see enough without even trying: chips of concrete, flakes of rust, bits of coal, dirty tissues, an old cracked and stained plastic bedpan, piles of cigarette butts, and gritty dust bunnies the size of tumbleweeds. It gave me the creeps. I wouldn't have been at all surprised if little green men had come marching out of there.

Our rooms didn't have telephones (like we could make a phone call without help anyway), or TVs (like there was anything in English we could watch since BBC had been banned in China and only the rich people who lived in the foreigner's compound got CNN), so we read a lot. Every night, after flushing my supper down the toilet, I went down to Justin's room and entertained us by reading James Herriot books aloud until bedtime.

One night, upon returning to my own room, I flipped on the overhead light as I walked through the door and a rat (yes, that's right, I said *rat*) the size of a small dog bolted out from under my bed. He scampered across my slippered feet, dashed into the bathroom, and scurried off to safety through the doorless cupboard under the ancient bathtub.

I shrieked.

I was not actually afraid of the rat—I'd gotten used to them by then, they were everywhere in Chengdu—but I didn't really think one belonged in my hospital room, and I was terrified of dirty needles and Chinese rabies shots.

I slammed the bathroom door shut fast, then hurriedly stuffed some extra quilt batting that had been hidden in a nearby closet into the three-inch crack under the door. Then, hoping that the rat wouldn't come out of its hiding place if my room wasn't dark, I left the lights on that whole night long.

At dawn I went looking for Dr. Twelve.

"There's a rat in my bathroom," I said.

"You want go bass-room?" he asked.

"No, there's a great big rat in my bathroom," I said.

Bewildered, he shook his head. That was a sure sign that the *ting bu dongs* were coming. "*Ting bu dong, ting bu dong,*" he said, saying it louder the second time, as if that would help a stupid foreigner like me understand him better.

"A rat," I said. "You know, RAT. R-A-T. RAT. There's a great big rat in my bathroom." I drew a rat in the air with my fingers.

"Ting bu dong, ting bu dong," he said.

"Rat, rat," I repeated. "You know, BIIGGG RAATTT." I stretched out the words, emphasizing them, thinking it might help him understand. I even tried to make a rat face. I wrinkled up my nose and curled up my lip. I chomped my teeth up and down and showed my fangs. I made some scary hissing noises and stuck my claws in his face. I was desperate to make him understand.

Dr. Twelve looked at me like he either thought I was on drugs or maybe he thought I needed some better drugs. He looked at me kindly, pityingly, shook his handsome young head once more and said, *"Ting bu dong, ting bu dong!"*

Well, since the visuals obviously weren't working, I let the rat face go and offered sweetly: "Can you please have someone set a trap?"

"Ting bu dong, ting bu dong," he said.

I was getting nowhere fast, but by now I'd been in China almost six months, and I was used to getting nowhere fast. However, I'd learned one or two useful things during that time, and one of the most foolproof things I'd learned was that the pen was mightier than the sword. If normal spoken English didn't work, and good old Chinglish didn't work, the trick was to write it down. The Chinese could read the written English word like they'd been born to it. Written in Chinglish, that is.

I picked up Dr. Twelve's pen and prescription pad off his desk and wrote "RAT IN BATHROOM, PLEASE MAKE TRAP" on it. I handed him the note. He studied it for a really long time. He turned it all the way around twice, then upside down and right side up three or four times. After ages and ages (about three minutes that seemed like thirty), he began scribbling some Chinese underneath the English. Then he picked up an also brand-new English-Chinese dictionary, checked everything twice, and scribbled some more.

Finally, benevolently, he took a deep breath, looked up, and blinked his big brown cow-eyes at me. With the deepest level of sincerity, patience and compassion I have ever heard in a single human voice, he said, "This hospital no have rat trap."

Now, I have a real low tolerance for ignorance and I can be a real bitch sometimes. I had this incredibly overpowering urge to get right in his face and scream, "Well, go buy one stupid!" because, in spite of the more than three hundred thirty-three items on my *Essential Things You Can't Buy in Chengdu* list (Dr Pepper, cottage cheese, Mounds bars and Playtex tampons in the pink box, just to name a few), a rat trap was one of the things I knew you *could* buy in Chengdu. Justin had just bought me one the week before so that we could try to catch the rat in our apartment.

But it was impossible to fight with that kind of Chinese logic. "This hospital no have rat trap," he had said.

I give up.

They always won.

"*Mei wan ti*," I mumbled. No problem.

Put in my proper spoiled American place, I crawled, humiliated and beaten, back down the hall to my room.

I was still really scared of getting bitten, however; yet I knew I couldn't avoid going into my own bathroom where, I feared, the rat still was. But I had to flush my food, and I could hardly sneak down to Justin's room with a tray of uneaten hospital food balanced on one arm and an IV on a stand attached the other three times a day. I decided that if I kept the rat full and fat and happy it just might stay in its cupboard under the ancient bathtub and out from under my bed (or, worse, on top of my bed with me), so I took to leaving it slimy goodies on the bathroom floor before flushing my food. And, of course, sometimes I had to go in there for other reasons, too.

Now for some unfathomable reason, the Chinese like to pull their toilet paper from the middle of the roll rather than the outside like normal people do in civilized countries, so they always take the cardboard center out. They don't need that cardboard thingy in there anyway, since most Chinese bathrooms aren't supplied with such amenities as toilet paper holders. Most of them, in fact, aren't even supplied with such amenities as toilet paper. But if you happen to be lucky enough to find a Chinese bathroom complete with toilet paper, I can promise you that it won't be hanging from a toilet paper holder neatly mounted to the wall. If it's a squatty potty, the toilet paper will be that wet gray lump on the floor sopping up a puddle of who-knows-what. If it's a sit-down, the toilet paper will be that sooty gray lump behind you, above the seat, lying sideways on the top of the toilet tank.

I was lucky, because my hospital bathroom—being that it was in the VIP wing and all—came complete with not only a sit-down toilet but its own toilet paper, too. And a kind and considerate nurse had even removed the cardboard center for me. The rat was lucky, too because, unbeknownst to me, that gave it a warm and soft cushy place in which to take its afternoon nap.

The afternoon of the day after I'd asked Dr. Twelve to set a trap and catch the rat, my IV and I hobbled into my bathroom to pee. Finished, I tried not to dislodge the needle or knock the bottle off the stand as I cranked my right arm around behind me and blindly groped for the soft, cushy roll of toilet paper I knew was lying on the tank.

The rat, to be sure, did not appreciate being so rudely awakened in the middle of its afternoon nap. Startled from its slumber, it squealed loudly, then skittered out from the center of the toilet paper roll. It ran up my arm, across my back, over my right shoulder, across my boob, down my chest, stomach and abdomen and landed on my bare and naked lap. Confused and disoriented, it teetered there for half a second, shook its fuzzy little head once or twice, then clawed its way across my bare and shaking thigh to the edge of my knee. Cautious now, it looked out over that human precipice, made its decision, and jumped. That rat hit that cold, clammy, grimy tile floor with a splat, skidded a couple of times like a dog on linoleum, and scampered off to safety under the ancient bathtub.

All I can say is that it was a damn good thing I was still sitting on the pot, because it scared the ever-livin' shit right out of me.

Thank God, it didn't bite.

That rat even made me famous. Years later, new foreigners in Chengdu were still coming up to me and asking me if I'd ever heard the story about the American woman who'd gone into the hospital and found a rat in her bathroom.

Yeah, I'd heard about that, all right, you bet.

Ha, ha, ha.

☯   ☯   ☯

Justin and I were each in the hospital for a week, and then we were both sent home with clean bills of health. I never saw the rat again, and although the conditions in the hospital were abhorrent, I felt like I'd received pretty good care. The Chinese dread the idea of a *lao wai* dying on them and, everything being relative, they'd gone out of their way to make sure I was comfortable and well-cared for. Justin, unfortunately, didn't fare quite so well. By the time he was released, two days after me, his hands and arms were yellow, black and blue, swollen to three times their normal size. The nurses, he said, had trouble getting his IVs in. Pulling on a shirt was sheer agony, he told me, and his hands hurt so badly he couldn't even stand the air to touch them. And although the bronchitis and lung infection were gone, it took several more weeks for his swollen limbs to heal.

But in spite of all the culture shock we'd experienced during that first six months, things were looking up. Spring was, finally, in the air. The grass was turning green. There were buds on the trees. A few flowers were blooming. Once in a while a lone bird chirped. And the sun—a misty white ball floating around in a gray-white sky—had actually shone for half a day. The grand opening ceremony of Sidney's new factory, which Justin had virtually built and set up, was only a week away, so corporate glory was at hand.

But I missed my rat, and all the birds I'd collected had flown away while I was in the hospital. When Justin and I had left the States, we'd had to find good homes for all our dogs and cats and horses and birds and cars and stuff, and it had broken my heart. When we got to Chengdu, we decided not to get another pet, because we thought that we would have to leave it behind when we moved back home to America. I couldn't bear the thought of giving a dog or a cat away to some local who would probably serve it center-table with an apple stuffed in its mouth or scald it to death in a hot pot. The few birds we'd kept had all flown off to freedom in the wild purple-gray yonder that supposedly passed for sky in Chengdu because I couldn't stand keeping them in cages. I missed having a pet so badly that I'd even threatened to bring the rat home from the hospital with me, since I couldn't have a dog, but Justin and Sidney had both forbidden it.

About a month after we got out of the hospital, Justin came home with a puppy.

He looked just like a Tribble. (The puppy, not Justin.)

Lovely.

I love animals.

"Take it back," I said. "I don't want it."

"Why not?" asked Justin.

"Because I can't bear to leave it," I said.

"We'll take him with us," Justin said. "Wherever we go, whatever we do, we'll take him with us."

"Even when we leave the country?"

"He goes."

"That costs money."

"I'll pay."

"Promise?"

"Promise."

Then, exactly one year later, Justin came home with a kitten.

"Take it back," I said. "I don't want it."

"Why not?" asked Justin.

"Because I can't bear to leave it," I said.

"We'll take her with us," he said. "Wherever we go, whatever we do, we'll take her with us."

"Even when we leave the country?"

"She goes."

"That costs money."

"I'll pay."

"Promise?"

"Promise."

And he did. When we moved to Thailand for a year, Toto (well, duh, since we weren't in Kansas or Nebraska or wherever it was anymore I couldn't possibly have named that dog anything else, now, could I?) and Tequila Sunrise (because the sun never shone in Chengdu) went with us. When we moved back to China a year later, Toto and Tequila moved back with us. Toto even has a little navy-blue book issued by the Chinese government with his picture in it and everything. It looks just like a little doggie passport. Tequila didn't need a little kitty passport though, just some special Immigration papers.

And even when we moved back to the States, Justin paid for them to come too, just like he always said he would (and it wasn't cheap, either).

Jeez, ya just gotta love a guy like that.

Chapter 7
Politics at Play

"I understand what you're saying," the U. S. Counsel General said, "but drinking is such a big part of expatriate life." It was during a Fourth of July Party planning committee meeting, and he was responding to a question I had just asked.

And he acted like I really ought to have known better.

And it really pissed me off.

☯   ☯   ☯

The American Consulate hosted two Independence Day parties each year. The official Officials' Party was held during the week, on official U.S. government time, and the Everybody Else's Party was held over the weekend, on regular people's time.

The official Officials' Party was by invitation only, and attended by high-ranking American bureaucrats and diplomats and VIPs and CEOs only. The high-ranking Chinese bureaucrats and diplomats and VIPs and CEOs who had been invited only attended if they knew for certain that their exact American counterpart would also be in attendance. Otherwise, they boycotted—it was an issue of face. The official Officials' Party was held on U.S. government time on U.S. government property and paid for with U.S. government funds.

At the official Officials' Party, all the really important people from the American Consulate stood around all afternoon on company time, collected their hardship pay, drank free beer, free wine and free champagne and ate free hors-d'oeuvres and free $2,500.00-paid-for-with-U.S.-tax-dollars Independence Day cake.

Also at the official Officials' Party, all the really important people from the American community in Chengdu stood around all afternoon on company time, collected their six-figure incomes from their big corporations, drank free beer, free wine and free champagne and ate free hors-d'oeuvres and free $2,500.00-paid-for-with-U.S.-tax-dollars Independence Day cake.

The $2,500.00-paid-for-with-U.S.-tax-dollars Independence Day cake was special-ordered, special-made and always shaped like the Lincoln Memorial, the White House, the Capitol Building, or some other important Washington landmark.

It was the epitome of American tax dollars at work.

Go figure.

The reason for the official Officials' Party was for the Americans to play be-nice with all the Chinese bureaucrats and diplomats and VIPs and CEOs, which was a really, really tricky thing to do in communist China at a party that celebrated an American holiday that celebrated democracy and freedom and personal liberties.

The Everybody Else's Party was the real people's party, the one everybody else attended, the one everybody looked forward to all year long. It was usually held on a Saturday, which gave everybody time to recover from their hangovers on Sunday, before they had to go back to work on Monday. It was undeniably the best party and the biggest blowout of the year. Chengdu's expat population was relatively small, so *everybody* came to the Everybody Else's Party, not just the Americans. It was the only time that the dividing social lines of the warring expat factions ever came crashing down. Once a year, on the Fourth of July, everybody just kicked back and had a good time. On that day, even the Brits forgot to be mad at us for winning the war in the first place.

It was awesome.

Funds were limited, however, due to budget cuts back over in good ol' Washington, D.C. and the price of the official Officials' Party champagne and $2,500.00-paid-for-with-U.S.-tax-dollars Independence Day cake and all. So the Everybody Else's Party, which was supposedly hosted by the American Consulate, was actually co-hosted by the Consulate and the Sichuan-American Chamber of Commerce (AmCham). But AmCham, being a relatively new organization at the time, didn't have a lot of members yet and therefore not a lot of money their coffers either, so both groups counted on many of the big international corporations doing business in Chengdu for donations. All the biggies—Kentucky Fried Chicken, Coca-Cola, Pepsi, Boeing/McDonnell Douglas, FedEx, Kodak, Dragon Air, Philip Morris—contributed. Some provided the food and drink, some gave away promotional items, and others simply kicked in cash.

Then one year, the all-knowing-powers-that-be back over in good ol' Washington, D.C. declared that cigarettes were an evil weed and that all tobacco products and tobacco-related paraphernalia would be banned (their exact words, according to the Counsel General, were "strongly discouraged") from all official and semi-official U.S. government functions worldwide.

Of all the party sponsors, Philip Morris was the biggest. Without them, there would be no party.

And Philip Morris, bless their nicotine-laden hearts, didn't just give away free cartons of cigarettes and Marlboro Man key chains and belt buckles and refrigerator magnets and pins and hats and cool stuff like that at the party, they also kicked in beaucoup bucks so that we could have a party in the first place.

Now, before you go jumping onto your anti-smoking bandwagon in support of this U.S. government worldwide ban on smoking, and before you go beating up on good ol' Philip Morris for being such a capitalist, you just try to remember that China is a different country, with a different culture and a different set of rules. Offering a cigarette to someone in China is considered an act of friendship, kind of like offering up a toast is in the West. Like it or not, you can't do business in China without cigarettes; it's a fact. In China, even people who don't smoke, smoke, just to be friendly, just to get *guanxi* ("*guanxi*" I'll explain later), and just to do business. People who don't smoke carry packs of cigarettes around, just to be friendly, just to get *guanxi* and just to do business. Everybody smokes in China. Everywhere. On elevators, in department stores, at the temples, on the buses, in the taxis, at the movies, at the opera, at the hospital. Yes, even at the hospital. Learn to put up with it or go home.

Justin always said it was the only way to do business in China.

I think it's population control.

But lucky for us that year, the party wouldn't have to be cancelled after all, because Philip Morris had just acquired Kraft Foods and Miller beer.

So the Fourth of July Party planning committee (present company excluded) decided that they'd just tell (order) good ol' Philip Morris to leave their evil old weeds at home, to leave their evil old weed-promoting paraphernalia at home, but please, of course, not to forget to bring the free beer.

And oh yeah, please, of course, not to forget to bring that thirty thousand *renminbi* (~ $3,600.00 U.S.) they'd promised to give us, either.

Bloody bureaucrats.

Fucking hypocrites.

It really pissed me off.

So I asked the Counsel General why Uncle Sam thought it was okay to get shit-faced on free booze at U.S. government parties on U.S. government property on U.S. government time, but it wasn't okay to smoke or get a free key chain. That was when he told me, in his superior, all-knowing, wise and wonderful diplomat's way, that it was because "drinking was such a big part of expatriate life."

Well, that explained it.

Go figure.

Then he gave me a look—*that look*—the one that said, really, Desi, you ought to know better, and just who the hell do you think you are, anyway, asking such a silly question, or bringing up such a delicate matter, in the first place?

Well, I didn't know better back then.

I don't know better now.

And to this day I still don't understand.
Since when is there a law against Marlboro Man key chains?
Or Marlboro cigarettes, for that matter.
Doesn't booze kill people, too?
Wasn't Prohibition abolished?
Sometimes there's more freedom in China.
That's really scary.
Need I say more?

Chapter 8
Expats Under Glass

Foreigners in Chengdu were always making friends with people they wouldn't walk across the street to spit on back home.

The corporate clique didn't associate with the lowlifes (foreign teachers and students).

The Consulate clique didn't socialize outside the Foreign Service, the CIA or the Peace Corps.

The Sichuan-American Chamber of Commerce was simply an entity unto itself.

The expat community-at-large was constantly fighting over the kinds of runs that the Chengdu Panda Hash House Harriers (the international social running club for runners with a drinking problem or drinkers with a running problem or whatever it is) should host—traditional (which meant lots of beer and dirty words) vs. family-oriented (which meant no beer and no dirty words).

And nobody liked being seen out in public with the missionaries.

The battle lines were clearly drawn.

I was caught right smack dab in the middle of this intricate network of overseas society vipers.

It was a most perfectly fascinating place to be.

I was Justin's fluff: an expat corporate wife.

I was a lowlife: an American English teacher.

I was not a member of the Foreign Service, the CIA or the Peace Corps, but I was an American citizen, and therefore found it necessary to visit the Consulate and socialize with the Consulate clique (and no doubt much to their dismay) from time to time.

I was a founding member of the Chengdu Panda Hash House Harriers (and fighting for the traditional side).

I was a board member of AmCham (and I, too, have been called "an entity unto myself" on occasion).

And I didn't particularly like being seen out in public with the Bible-thumpers, because I hated being photographed by the Public Security Bureau, but a couple of the missionaries truly acted more like real people than many of the other foreigners who lived in Chengdu, so sometimes I hung out with one or two of them, too, just to be nice.

Justin often said that back home in America, whenever he'd walked into a room full of people, he had always felt like the strangest person there, but that in China, every time he walked into a room full of foreigners, he always felt like the most normal person there.

That was pretty scary, because Justin's a pretty weird guy.

Expat parties were a joke, always complete with one or two token Chinese, usually beautiful young girls attached to middle-aged men twenty or thirty years their senior. Nine times out of ten, good old mom and the kids were stashed away back home in their own countries, basking in the comforts of the civilized Western world, while supposedly poor old dear old dad was stuck over in poor old primitive China slaving away earning the big bucks for the good of the family. Then, when good old mom and the kids came over to China for their token yuppie culture trips, or for the summer, or to check up on poor old dear old dad, or whatever, the Chinese girlfriends would all disappear into the woodwork (usually), and all the rest of us would have to make nice with good old mom and the kids and make them feel welcome and make them feel at home and pretend we'd never met any of poor old dear old dad's Chinese girlfriends.

Ugh.

And the ladies' daytime get-togethers seemed like an absolute farce to me, or perhaps their upper-class world was simply beyond the scope of my countrified horizons. They sat around and talked about their kids, and their token yuppie culture trips to Beijing and Shanghai and Bangkok and Hong Kong and Tibet, and whether or not their new drapes matched their new furniture and their new furniture matched their new carpet in their new Chinese European-style villas in Chengdu (which was all being paid for, lock, stock and barrel, by their husband's companies). Then they sat around and talked about whether or not their new drapes matched their new furniture and their new furniture matched their new carpet in their fancy, corporately-correct, executive-style new houses back home, too. They talked about their Western medicines and their operations and flying back home to the civilized world just to get a prescription filled. A token yuppie culture trip for me consisted of a trip to the *mai cai* or, if I was extremely lucky, a three hour ride up to the mountains of Wo Long to visit the pandas. I didn't have any kids, my "drapes" were homemade gingham curtains (made of fabric I'd bought at the *mai cai* and sewed together on my brand new Chinese department-store-bought non-electric treadle sewing machine), Sidney had picked out all my furniture before I'd even got there, and I'd ripped up all the carpet in my seventh-floor executive penthouse company *condomimium* because it smelled like dirty underwear. It seemed to me that most of the expat corporate fluff sat around all day and complained about having nothing to do, but anytime anybody ever organized an activity, nobody ever showed up. Prozac bored me.

So sitting around at coffee klatches or doing Long Island Iced Tea lunches with a bunch of women I didn't know very well but knew well enough to know I had nothing in common with was not at the top of my list of fun things to do. And, on the very rare and usually obligatory occasions (and sometimes just out of morbid curiosity) when I did have to attend one of these lovely little ladies' daytime drinking functions, I always managed to do, say and wear the wrong thing.

Sometimes on purpose.

Meeooowwww.

But mostly I didn't attend these lovely little ladies' daytime drinking functions because I was terrified that one day I might have to host one.

The truth was that these women intimidated me. I didn't know how to throw a corporate dinner party, I didn't live like them in the rich people's compound, we didn't get CNN so I had no idea what was going on out in the rest of the world, and my husband didn't make a six-figure income. I had a dog that had accidents on the floor and a cat that was stone-deaf, both of whom did exactly as they pleased exactly when they pleased. Our apartment was seven flights up—no elevator, freezing cold in winter, sweltering hot in summer. My refrigerator was filled with beer, and in my house, smoking was allowed. I didn't have an oven so I couldn't bake cookies (like I would know how to in the first place), my melon balls always looked like they needed air, and my punch tasted like traditional Chinese medicine. The really yucky kind.

Yet even though most of my domestic skills left quite a lot to be desired, I was damn good at a couple of other things, and one of those things was collecting information that helped make expat life in China easier. I had this great collection of lists—important addresses and food names and typical questions and local prices—all written down in both Chinese (for them) and English (for me). I could get into a taxi and go anywhere I wanted anytime I wanted, and I didn't even have to speak the language. I knew which store sold the cheese, which store sold the butter, which store sold the American-style egg noodles, and which store sold the real ice cream. I knew where to get the root beer, the Diet Coke and the ginger ale. Best of all, I knew where all the civilized toilets were.

Eventually, the American Consulate got wind of this, and they started giving out my phone number (with my permission) to any foreigners they knew were coming into town. Unofficially (and unintentionally), I became Chengdu's expat welcome wagon lady. Now most of the foreigners moving into town, and even the occasional tourist, started calling me up for help. I was constantly escorting new resident *lao wais* (both male and female) to the *mai cai*, handing out copies of all my lists, and sharing all the useful tidbits of information I'd gathered—like where the best sit-down toilets were.

Then one day, quite by accident, I discovered that I was famous. On the way to the *mai cai*, and quite out of the blue, a European woman I'd just met asked me if I'd ever heard the rumor about the American woman who'd spent a week in a Chengdu hospital with a rat in her bathroom.

I was so surprised that at first I didn't know what to say. The whole rat-in-the-hospital thing had happened more than a year earlier. "Yeah, I heard about that," I finally managed.

She asked me if it was true.

"Yeah, it's true," I said.

She asked me how I knew.

"I was there," I said.

She asked me what I meant by "there"—had I gone to visit my friend?

"Not exactly," I said.

"Well, then," she insisted, "how do you know it's true?"

I figured it was best just to give it to her straight, even though she was from one of those upper-class European countries where they think all Americans are heathens. "Well," I said, "probably because the first time I seen that rat, he was running out from under my bed and across my feet, and the second time I seen that rat, he was sleeping in the toilet paper roll, but he woke up and ran across my shoulder when I grabbed some—"

She shrieked, eyes wide, and put her hand to her mouth in shock. She looked so horrified that I didn't have the heart to finish the story. She gasped and cried, "Are you serious?"

"Yeah, I'm serious," I said, deadpan. "But that was nuthin'. Just wait 'til you see the *mai cai.*"

Yeah, I can be a real bitch sometimes.

Ha, ha, ha.

She turned and ran straight for the isolated, insulated sanctuary of her Chinese European-style villa in the rich people's compound, and I didn't see much of her after that.

A couple of weeks later, when I was in obligatory attendance at a Consulate-sponsored expat get-together, one of the more politically appropriate American diplomats cornered me.

"You know, Desi," he said, with that highfalutin air they all learned in college, "you really shouldn't go around spreading rumors about rats running about in hospital rooms."

Excuse me?

Rumors?

What rumors?

I hadn't been spreading any rumors.

I was there.

It wasn't a rumor.

It was the truth.

It was my hospital room and my rat.

And I told him so.

Emphatically.

He did not appear to appreciate being so enlightened.

He said that I should know better.

He said that I shouldn't go around spreading such dreadful stories.

Maybe the U.S. government just didn't like me telling the truth.

Go figure.

☯   ☯   ☯

I was an expatriate social outcast and I knew it, but I really didn't care. I'd had enough of the foreign community's two-faced, backstabbing, lying, cheating, saving face and giving face I'll-be-friends-with-you-here-because-there's-nobody-else-to-be-friends-with-but-if-I-was-back-home-I-wouldn't-walk-across-the-street-to-spit-on-you games.

If you didn't work you were expected to play, so I went out and got myself a job.

Chapter 9

Teaching English Ain't Just About Good Grammar

Teaching English not only seemed like a good and graceful way to get out of hosting luncheons and making nice with the fluff, it also seemed like the best way to feed my pet obsession: getting to know the natives.

I was also sick to death of listening to Chinese people who talked like a dictionary, and I had made it my personal mission in life to do something about it. The Chinese still believed that memorization was the best way to learn, so they would read their English-Chinese dictionaries and their Chinese-English dictionaries and their English grammar books and memorize them from cover to cover. Then, to every foreigner they met, they would recite useful phrases like, "Hello, how are you?" or "Nice to meet you." Trouble was, these useful phrases were not really useful at all because:

(1) If they didn't get what was considered the correct response according to whatever badly-written English language book they'd memorized, they'd get all confused and flustered and stuck and wouldn't know what to say next, and

(2) They were always saying "Hello, how are you?" and "Nice to meet you" to people they hadn't even met yet.

I'd heard that Sichuan Union University was looking for warm bodies to teach English in their intensive language training center, so I fixed up my résumé, rode my bicycle on over and applied.

My first and only interview went something like this:

Mr. Yang, the man in charge, gave my résumé a perfunctory glance, peered at me from over the top of his bifocals and asked, "Have you ever taught English before?" Gray light glinted off the top of his shiny, bald head.

"Nope," I said. "I never taught English before and I don't know nuthin' about grammar, so if you're lookin' for a grammar teacher, I ain't it. I teach *communication*, not grammar." I smiled sweetly and gave him what I hoped was an "I dare you to challenge me on that one" look.

He hired me on the spot.

☯   ☯   ☯

Mr. Yang warned me not to break any Chinese laws or preach religion during class, something he insisted qualified as breaking the law. There were a lot of missionaries pretending to be English teachers in China, so I understood why he'd mentioned it, but Bible-thumping was never my intention. I was there to teach, not preach. Then he gave me a couple of battered old pirated paperback textbooks—Sino-American Culture and Oral Communication (both about vintage 1963)—and sent me upstairs to meet my first class.

So much for foreign teacher's orientation.

☯   ☯   ☯

I was terrified as I climbed the dusty old cement stairs to Room 301. Although Nebraska Midwestern Hillbilly American English was my native language, I wondered if I could really pull something like this off. Another harebrained scheme had gotten me into another fix and now, here I was, about to start pretending to be an English teacher in one of Chengdu's finest universities.

Why was I always doing this to myself?

Trembling, heart pounding, I finally reached the dirty urine-yellow-colored door of Room 301, pushed it open and stepped into my future as an English teacher in the People's Republic of China.

The dank and gloomy classroom where I would end up spending a lot of my time for the next few years was a depressing sight indeed. Two of the walls were covered with that same lifeless chalky-blue stuff the Chinese call paint that dusted the interior of every other Chinese building I'd ever been in. Thick black mold spread out from all four corners of the ceiling and ran down the walls like intricate inkblot tests. A row of cracked and broken windows ran along the far wall. Every pane of glass was coated with that same grimy, gritty, gray coal-dust film that permeated everything in Chengdu (grass, leaves, whole trees, food, water, birds, air, people). A huge old black-slate chalkboard—so tall I'd never reach its top—ran the entire length of the wall at the front of the room above a raised wooden platform on which sat a rickety old teacher's podium.

And thirty-three very expectant Oriental faces stared out at me, wide-eyed with wonder.

The Great White Goddess had come to share the secret to the universe: English.

They all looked like that was what they thought, anyway.

WOW.

Go figure.

But I was overwhelmed, and really, really scared; on the verge of hyperventilating. I didn't know the first thing about teaching English, or English communication, or whatever, but I did know that it just wouldn't do for their new foreign teacher to run screaming from the room in terror—we'd all lose face. I dropped my backpack and my books onto the rickety old podium, took a deep breath, or two, or maybe it was three, counted to ten, or maybe it was twenty, and faced my students for the very first time.

But I really had no clue as to how to begin.

At that point (about thirty seconds into the room), I really didn't care if I lost face.

And, at that moment, I really didn't care if they lost face, either.

I wanted to go home.

To Nebraska.

But I was frozen to the spot.

So I took another deep breath, or two, or maybe it was three, counted to ten, or maybe it was twenty, and thought, OK, how hard can this be?

I could speak English, so I could teach it, right?

If I couldn't baffle them with bullshit, I could dazzle them with brilliance, right?

And if that didn't work, I could just do what the Chinese always did and hide behind the excuse of *ting bu dong, ting bu dong*, right?

Because the way I saw it, I only had two choices: I could become full-time fluff, or I could handle this teaching thing.

I chose the latter.

So I opened my mouth to say something brilliant and enlightening, but nothing came out. Not a peep or a squeak. My throat was dry, my tongue was swollen, I was still very nervous and they were all still staring at me. To cover my unease, I grabbed a piece of chalk from off the top of the podium, turned around and, hand trembling, filled the blackboard with great big bold white letters:

Desĩree Dĩane Downey

I wrote, just like that, with a little heart dotting each *i*, just to make it more interesting.

I took another deep breath, swallowed the lump in my throat, mustered up some courage and turned back around to face my students. I put on my best I-know-what-I'm-doing imitation teacher's voice, and slowly read the words I'd written on the board out loud:

"Dez-uh-reeee Dye-aynne Dow-ah-ney."

I underlined each word for emphasis as I spoke and, in spite of that old Nebraska twang, I managed to enunciate each syllable to perfection.

All the people in the room broke out into an agitated giggle. They all turned collectively beet red, looked thoroughly confused and immediately snatched up all their English-Chinese dictionaries. There was a frantic flipping of pages (traditional book form) and a frenzied blipping of keys (high-tech electronic form), and then they all just stopped what they were doing and gave me THAT LOOK. They appeared to be in a state of TOTAL CONFUSION.

"Can you speak more slowly?" asked a pretty little thing in the second row.

"*Ting bu dong, ting bu dong*" several students muttered, simultaneously.

"*Lao wai* speak English?" I heard another whisper.

"Is not in dictionary," someone else said.

Well, of course it wasn't in their dictionaries.

Good God, that was my name.

I was certainly off to a rip-roaring start if I couldn't even teach them my name.

"My name," I said. "That's my name. 'Desiree Diane Downey' is my name."

"What you want us call you?" asked the pretty little thing in the second row.

"Desi," I said. "Everybody just calls me Desi."

"Mmmm…, Miss Daisy, yes?" she said, rolling it around on her tongue. Then she smiled and asked, "Like flower, yes?"

Ooooh, I like that, I thought. You can be my favorite. "Yeah, that's right," I said. Of course I wouldn't correct her in front of all her classmates and make her lose face.

"I have American name," she continued. "I am Rainbow. I come from Tibet. Where do you come from?"

I started to relax (maybe this wouldn't be so hard after all), smiled back at her and said, "Nebraska. I come from Nebraska."

"Alaska?" asked a flat-faced young man in the back row.

"No, not Alaska," I answered. "Nuh-brass-ka."

"Alaska very cold, yes?" he asked.

"No, not Alaska," I repeated, "Nuh-brass-ka." I turned back to the blackboard, erased my name with a lopsided eraser older than dirt, and sketched a squiggly square thing with a couple of lumps on it—what was theoretically a map of America—in its place.

"This is America," I said. Near the center of the squiggly square thing I drew a great big rectangle and highlighted it with a great big star. "And this…" I said, stabbing at the star and breaking the chalk, "is Nuh-brass-ka."

Then I wrote:

N E B R A S K A

in great big bold white letters under the great big rectangle with the great big star.

"This is where I come from," I continued. "Nuh-brass-ka. I used to be a farmer. I grew corn and rode horses in America."

"Like a peasant?" Rainbow asked.

(In China, all peasants are farmers, or all farmers are peasants, or something like that—I never did quite figure it out.)

"Well, it's not exactly the same thing," I said, then tried to explain that farming in America was a highly respected profession. "Americans do not always want to live in the cities. Some Americans want to live in the countryside. Many Americans even *want* to be farmers."

I could tell from the looks on their incredulous faces that they didn't believe me.

"But all farmers are poor," said the student who'd asked me if Nebraska was Alaska, "and all Americans are rich."

To them, it made perfect sense: if all peasants were farmers and all farmers were poor and all Americans were rich *why on earth would anybody want to be a peasant farmer and stay out in the countryside and be poor when they could move into the city and get rich?*

Forty acres and a mule just didn't compute.

So there I was, little more than a quarter of an hour into my very first lesson disguised as an English teacher in the People's Republic of China, and off to a great start. If I couldn't even teach them my name and the name of my state, how was I going to teach them the difference between a countable and an uncountable noun?

It was definitely time to go with something simple and more basic. I decided to try the *how-are-you?* thing.

"How are y'all?" I asked.

Flip, flap.

Blip, blap.

And then, again, TOTAL CONFUSION.

Ting bu dong, ting bu dong.

"Is not in dictionary," Rainbow said.

What?

Whaddya mean "y'all" is not in the dictionary?

And so what?

Neither is "Desiree Diane Downey."

That don't mean they ain't words.

Does it?

Yes, it does.

At least in China it does.

That was my first lesson.

Go figure.

Chapter 10
It's All in the Name

All Chinese people do not look alike, although it's a known fact that they think all foreigners do. I knew each student's face, but not their name, and I could hardly spend the entire semester pointing at any given one and calling out "Hey-you-with-the-black-hair!" Assigning each one a number had just seemed way too proletarian.

I had asked them to stand up and introduce themselves, but it didn't take long for me to realize that there wasn't a snowball's chance in all the eighteen levels of hell that I was ever gonna be able to pronounce any of their Chinese names. "Song" and "Wang" and "Wong" and "Huang" and "Zhang" and "Zhan" may look easy, but they're not. "Song" sounds like a mantra (a drawn out "soon" with a "g") and "Wang" and "Huang" are supposedly different, but they both sound exactly like "Wong" with an "o" except for the silent "H," which the Chinese can hear but the foreigners can't. "Zhang" with a "g" and "Zhan" without also sound absolutely identical, except for the silent "g" that the Chinese can also hear but the foreigners also can't. Plus, each name must be pronounced with exactly the right tone and exactly the right inflection, otherwise you might end up calling the guy named Mr. Ma (which means horse) Mr. Ma (which means leech).

I took little comfort in the fact that they couldn't say "Desi" and called me "Miss Daisy" instead.

I decided to give them each an American name, just like Sidney had done in his company. Taking an American name was a very popular thing to do among students of English in China, and I'd thought it was a little bit odd that most of them didn't already have American names to begin with anyway. I found out later that many of them did, actually, but either hadn't liked the teacher who'd given them the name or hadn't liked the name, so it became my job to assign new ones.

One day, I took an American baby names book I'd stolen from a leaving foreigner to class and held what I called the Great American Name-Giving Lesson. But since I didn't want to end up with a bad rap like all those other teachers who'd assigned all those names the students didn't like, I decided to let them choose their own names. I split the blackboard in half and wrote a bunch of girl's names from the baby names book on one side and boy's names on the other.

"Okay, pick," I said.

I'd figured this would be a piece of cake, but of course, it wasn't. The sounds of most American names—and nearly all of the ones I'd written on the board—were just too unfamiliar. My students had trouble with "R," "L," "M," "V" and "Th." They couldn't pronounce names with consonants at the end, like "Thomas, which became "Thomas-uh" or "Julian," which became "Julia"—okay for the girls, not so good for the boys. And they couldn't pronounce anything that was more than two syllables long. And once I got through the "How to spell?" and "How to say?" stuff I had to deal with the "What's mean?" stuff. If they didn't like the meaning, the name was history. After about an hour of this and only a couple of names chosen, I knew that I had better come up with a better idea, and fast.

It was then that I had another one of my infrequent, brilliant ideas.

The Chinese *love* American music and they *love* American movies. Why not let them pick celebrity names?

It worked.

For the most part.

Except for Tao.

Tao was tall for a Chinese man, and dark, and arrogant and square, except for his eyeballs, which popped out of his head like a fly's. He didn't walk, he strutted, and the first time I met him was when he sashayed into class, two weeks and ten minutes late one Thursday morning, smack-dab in the middle of one of my more profound lectures like the one about Americans wanting to be farmers and all farmers not being peasants or something.

"Hullo," he interrupted. "I am Tao. I am Chinese. I am proud to be Chinese. I love my government, I love my country and I don't want an American name. *You* may call me Tao." He thudded into a seat in the front row, just to the right of the rickety old teacher's podium, and glared at me with a look that said, I dare you, go ahead, I just dare you to challenge me.

So much for all that undying love, respect and devotion the Chinese have for their foreign teachers.

I smiled with what felt like was my very best I'm-the-teacher-and-I'm-in-charge-here condescending smile and said, "Ni howdy, Tao. Welcome to Sino-American culture class. *You* can call *me* Miss Daisy." Silently I breathed a prayer of thanks to God and Buddha too that "Tao" was a name I could pronounce.

For the rest of that semester, and for all the time that I knew him, Tao treated me like a real person, and an equal.

It was real nice not to be a *lao wai* anymore.

Chapter 11
American Life Is Not Like an American Movie

By the end of the Great American Name-Giving Lesson, I ended up with a class full of students named Michael and Jackson and Whitney and Houston, Kevin (*"Dance-with-a-Wolf"*), Arnold (*Future Soldier* a/k/a *"Terminator"*), Rocky (obvious), Scarlett and Rhett (*"Gone-with-Wind"*) and Romeo and Juliet (obvious).

I decided that they were definitely watching too many American movies.

The Chinese believe with all their hearts and souls that all American people live exactly like all American people do in all the American movies they watch. They believe with all their hearts and souls that if they study really hard and learn to speak English really good, they will be able to immigrate to America and immediately begin to live that way, too.

I believed with all my heart and soul that it was my sworn patriotic duty to dispel this ignorant myth.

"Do y'all like to watch American movies?" I asked my students one day.

"YES!" they roared.

"Do y'all think American life is just like an American movie?" I asked.

"YES!" they screamed.

"Do y'all like to watch Chinese movies?"

"NO!" they howled.

"Do y'all think Chinese life is just like a Chinese movie?"

"NO!" they bellowed.

"But you think American life is just like an American movie?"

"YES!" they screamed.

I sighed, shook my head at them sadly, picked up a brand new piece of chalk from the podium, turned to my buddy the blackboard and, in great big bold white letters, wrote:

IF CHINESE LIFE IS NOT LIKE A CHINESE MOVIE,
THEN WHY DO YOU THINK AMERICAN LIFE
IS LIKE AN AMERICAN MOVIE?

I was rewarded with dead silence.

Real fear.

And TOTAL CONFUSION.

But they were only pretending not to understand.

Ting bu dong, ting bu dong—what a load of crap, I thought.

They understood, all right—I could tell by the looks on their frightened faces.

They just didn't like what they understood very much.

"Well?" I demanded.

No answer.

"Well?" I stood before them, hands on hips, foot tapping, staring them down. "I'm waiting."

Still no answer.

I tapped a broken pencil against the podium. Click, click. Click, click. Click, click.

"I'm still waiting," I said.

Click, click. Click, click. Click, click.

No answer.

It was a Sino-American standoff.

The Great White Goddess, Holder of the Key to the Secret to the Universe, Purveyor of Knowledge, had just purveyed knowledge that nobody wanted.

Just who did I think I was, anyway?

But after a minute or two, I started to feel a little guilty. They were such a good group, and so grateful, even though they were so very innocent and naïve. I relented (a little).

"Okay," I said, "let's talk about *why* you think American life is like an American movie."

"Because everybody in America rich," said Mr. Alaska-Nebraska, who was now going by the name of Rocky.

"Why do you believe that?" I asked.

"Because can see in America-movie," he answered.

"Why do you believe that's like real life?" I asked.

He was very, very sure of himself. "Because I know everybody in America drive big car. I know everybody in America live big house. America life perfect."

"How do you know that?" I asked.

"Because can see in America-movie," he answered.

"Real people don't live like that," I said. "Chinese movies are not like real Chinese life and American movies are not like real American life. Why do you think we are so different from you?"

"Money," said Rocky.

Well, gee, there ya go.

It was perfectly logical.

The Great Greenback God to the rescue.

Of course.

That's what made us different.

All foreigners were rich, so all foreigners lived like that.

I just loved Chinese rationalizations.

In spite of the Hollywood delusions of my students (and the Chinese people in general) that all foreigners were rich and that American life was just like an American movie, and despite the fact that I suspected they were definitely watching too many American movies, sometimes I showed one during class. Theoretically, it was a good way to improve a student's English listening comprehension skills. Realistically, I thought the Chinese subtitles made it too easy for them.

So whenever I used a movie in class, I always obliterated the Chinese subtitles by taping paper over the bottom quarter of the TV screen. The idea was to force them to listen to the English and not just read the Chinese.

They shrieked and howled and carried on and sounded just like the Sichuan Opera.

They claimed that they couldn't understand the movies without the subtitles.

I claimed that they would never learn English if they spent their lives relying on subtitles.

They hated me for it.

The Buddhists say that whatever brings you joy will eventually bring you pain.

Ah, well…

Go figure.

Some of my students even thanked me for it later.

Chapter 12
Real People Don't Talk
Like That

English was no longer the forbidden language in China, and all the trappings of the bourgeois class, so previously and violently shunned, were no longer looked down upon by the Chinese masses. The days of book burnings, academic executions, public humiliations and rehabilitation of intellectuals by sending them off to the countryside to get dirt under their fingernails were ancient history.

English was the language of the outside world, the language of freedom and the ticket to a better life, and the young, modern Chinese were desperate to learn it, practice it and study it with a foreign teacher.

Unfortunately, however, learning it, practicing it and studying it didn't always mean comprehensive use of it; more often than not it simply meant memorization and recitation of it.

Sometimes I thought that Chinese students of English often took the idea of memorization and recitation just a little too far. At one graduation ceremony I attended, a student graduating with high honors got up on stage and, in front of about 1,200 Chinese people who only spoke Chinese, maybe a couple hundred Chinese students who spoke fair-to-middling English, and a mere dozen or so English-speaking foreigners, recited, from memory, verbatim, Lincoln's Gettysburg Address, from beginning to end. And I know he had no idea what any of it meant, because I asked him later. One of the school's directors had simply asked him to do it, he said, so he did.

And the whole idea of graduation in and of itself was a complete and total farce, because it didn't matter if the students had learned anything or not, if they'd paid their money, they got their certificates. Period. One student, who barely spoke any English at all, *and who had attended only one class during the entire semester*, showed up at school on graduation day, sauntered up to me just before the ceremonies began, and had the unmitigated audacity to ask me to help her with her U.S. visa application by helping her fill out the forms and then going with her to the American Consulate (I said no). She got her diploma anyway (and probably her visa, too). Another student, who had only been coming to class during the last week of the term, and who didn't understand and couldn't even answer the question "How are you?" during final oral exams had a very, very rich daddy, so she got her diploma anyway. When I complained to one of school's directors, he just smiled and shrugged and said, "They pay their money so, well, you know...."

But most Chinese students study very, very hard, try really, really hard, and are very, very grateful. Most of my pupils were so diligent in memorizing their textbooks, grammar books and dictionaries from cover to cover that it drove me crazy. They often used great big complex words I didn't even know. I'd have to secretly jot them down during class on a pad I kept on a shelf under the top of the rickety old podium just for that reason, and then run home later and look them up on the sly.

The problem, as I saw it anyway, was that every time a Chinese person heard an English word they didn't know, they shut off their brains and dived for their dictionaries. They didn't hear anything else that was said and, although the Chinese functional analytical ability often left quite a lot to be desired, they didn't even try to figure out the meaning of the word from the rest of the sentence. They all sounded just like Noah Webster, and it drove me crazy.

I finally forbid them from using their dictionaries during class. They didn't believe me, until I started confiscating every dictionary I saw during class, electronic or otherwise.

They shrieked and howled and carried on and sounded just like the Sichuan Opera.

They claimed that they couldn't understand English without their dictionaries.

I claimed that they would never learn to communicate naturally in English if they spent their lives relying on their dictionaries.

They claimed that they couldn't interview for a visa or a job as a translator or entrance into a foreign university without their dictionaries.

I claimed that if they were interviewing for a visa or a job as a translator or entrance into a foreign university they probably wouldn't get the visa or the job as a translator or accepted into the foreign university if they spent the whole interview looking up words their dictionaries.

They didn't believe me.

It was then that I had yet another one of my infrequent, brilliant ideas.

I simply pointed out to them that asking me the meaning of a word rather than looking it up in their dictionaries would give them more chances to practice their oral English.

That did the trick.

It was just a matter of motivating them.

The biggest problem I had with my students relying on their dictionaries and grammar books so much was that these texts often didn't teach them how to use the words correctly, or how to speak the language naturally.

They said "lost" when they meant "stolen" and "sentimental" when they meant "depressed." Instead of asking "Where are you from?" or "Are you cold?" they said things like, "Where do you come from?" and "Do you feel cold?"

"Real people don't talk like that," I told them.

They didn't believe me.

Their pronunciation was awful, too. They refused to stick their tongues out when they said a "th" word so "thank you" always came out "sank you." And for about the last twenty years, some idiot at one of the middle schools had been teaching all Chinese students to add "es" to the word "clothes," so it always came out as "clothes-zes." I spent a lot of time undoing that one, and I spent a lot of time on pronunciation in my classes.

Then there was the problem of how to nix their ridiculous obsession with what they called "useful phrases." Good God, I wondered, how useful was it to say "Nice to meet you" to someone they hadn't even met yet? How useful was it to ask, "Where do you come from?" when they didn't understand the answer?

I did not then and do not now believe that a useful phrase is useful if it cannot be followed up by intelligent, or even remotely interesting, conversation.

As their teacher, I felt it was my duty to teach them to *use* the English language, not to memorize it, rehearse it and recite it without comprehension.

And the textbooks were really awful, but there weren't any decent ones available, so most foreign teachers just used whatever the school provided, and tried to make the best of it.

All the textbooks I saw were always out of date, pirated, badly copied and full of obscure grammar rules, bad sentence syntax and ridiculous sample dialogues. I hated grammar, I hated syntax and I hated sample dialogue.

And most of the textbooks I saw advised students to simply approach anybody on the street who looked like an English-speaking foreign friend (translation: perfect stranger), and then gave a happy example of how a typical conversation should go:

STUDENT: "Hello, how are you?"

FOREIGN FRIEND: "Hello. I am fine, thank you, and you?"

S: "I am fine, thank you. Nice to meet you."

FF: "Nice to meet you, too."

S: "What is your name?"

FF: "My name is John. What is your name?"

S: "My name is Xiao Ma. Where do you come from?"

FF: "I come from America."

S: "How long have you been in China?"

FF: "I have been in China one month."

S: "How do you think about China?"

FF: "I like China very much."

S: "How do you think about Chinese food?"

FF: "I like Chinese food very much."

S: "Have you had your dinner?"

FF: "No, I have not had my dinner."

S: "I must go now. I have something to do. Goodbye."

FF: "Goodbye."

Good God, it was no wonder the Americans and the Chinese had so much trouble communicating with each other all the time.

"Real people don't talk like that," I told my students.

They didn't believe me.

Then there was grammar. I hated grammar. I tried to convince my students that the only reason they needed to learn the grammar rules was to break them.

I thought they didn't believe me.

One day we were doing countable and uncountable nouns. There was a list in the book, and I had asked them to read the words from the list and identify each noun as either countable or uncountable.

Book, movie, apple. Countable.

Furniture, information, equipment. Uncountable.

Et cetera.

Et cetera.

Money.

Money?

Money.

Countable or uncountable?

The book said: uncountable.

Laughing, and almost as if they were indeed all of one collective consciousness, albeit a happy, friendly one, in unison they shrieked: "Countable!"

Countable?

Countable.

I believed them.

Chapter 13
They Don't Really Eat That, Do They?

An ancient Chinese proverb says, *"Sichuan people are afraid of everything that is not hot."*

This was absolutely, positively true.

The Sichuanese smeared that repugnant, reeking *hua jiao* and *la jiao* all over everything they ate. Its caustic, fetid odor permeated their skin, their bodies, their hair, their clothing, their homes and their cars. It permeated the very air that we breathed. They dowsed their Kentucky Fried Chicken with it, and only God and Buddha too knew what they put into their pizzas.

Justin called Sichuan the "Land of a Billion Smells" but to me it had only one smell—that of a billion thousand-year-old rotten eggs festering in a pool of carbon monoxide, *hua jiao* and *la jiao*.

We found it impossible to convey to the Chinese that I was a vegetarian and that that meant that I ate *no meat* and *no fish*. Period. The Chinese just all automatically assumed that since all foreigners were rich, and since all rich people could afford to eat meat, they did, just because they could. The whole idea of a rich *lao wai* choosing not to eat meat or fish just didn't compute.

And Sidney, Justin's boss, was the worst one of all.

I was sitting in between Sidney and the visiting American vice president of THE COMPANY at a VIP dinner held in his honor one evening I'll never forget.

And neither did Sidney.

There were twelve or fifteen people in attendance besides me, Justin, Sidney, Mr. Wang of course, and the American VP, including several others also from the American office, a handful of Chinese dignitaries who were there simply to give Sidney big face, and three or four Chinese people who worked at the office or the factory in Chengdu.

It was a typical Sichuan banquet.

"Here, try this!" Sidney screamed, and shoved a chunk of turtle at me.

"Sidney, my wife is a vegetarian," Justin said for the umpteenth time.

"Here, drink this!" Sidney yelled, and pushed a glass of bloody red turtle bile at me.

"Sidney, my wife is a vegetarian," Justin said again for the umpteenth time.

"Here, try this!" Sidney screamed, and shoved a chunk of snake meat at me.

"Sidney, my wife doesn't eat meat," Justin reiterated.

"Here, drink this!" Sidney yelled, and pushed a glass of slimy green snake bile at me.

"Sidney, she doesn't like it," Justin said.

"You no like it?" Sidney bellowed. "Here, try this!" He stabbed his chopsticks toward a platter of what looked like goat guts and rat skulls.

Justin sighed. "Sidney, *please*. My wife only eats vegetables and tofu."

"*Dofu*? You want some *dofu*?" Sidney asked me.

Good God, yeah, that would be great, I thought. "Yeah, that would be great," I said.

Fifteen minutes later, a bowl of cold, greasy, mushy white stuff which was soaking in a pool of *hua jiao* and *la jiao* appeared in front of me, most of its contents obliterated by a layer of unidentifiable little bitty brown chunks of dog meat or who-knew-what. I couldn't stand the smell of it, and I couldn't stand the sight of it, so I quietly, discreetly pushed it out of the way.

The American VP seated next to me leaned over and whispered, "Is there something wrong with your tofu?"

"No, I'm just not really hungry," I answered. I was starving, but I knew better than to say something that might lose somebody big face.

Unfortunately, Sidney had seen me push the bowl away, too. He asked me the same question the VP had asked me, and got the same answer. Then somebody else at the table asked me, and then somebody else asked me again.

I continued to repeat that I was not hungry, but nobody at the table was buying it. And they just would not leave me alone about it. They harped on and on and on and on, and would not give it up.

Finally, I'd had enough. I didn't blame them, I didn't blame Sidney, and I didn't blame the restaurant, but I didn't want anybody to order me anything else (which would no doubt also be covered with disgusting little bits of who-knew-what). By now I truly wasn't hungry anymore, because I'd totally and completely lost my appetite. There was simply no way I was going to eat that slop, and I just wanted them to leave me alone. I mumbled something under my breath about not having ordered tofu covered with *hua jiao, la jiao* and unidentifiable little bitty brown chunks of dog meat—a remark intended to be heard only by the American VP sitting next to me who'd started it all in the first place—but unfortunately everyone sitting at the table clearly heard what I'd said. The American women looked shocked, the Chinese women looked shocked, the American VIPs—including the Taiwanese ones—looked shocked, and the Chinese dignitaries looked, at first, confused, then shocked. Sidney took it personally, blamed me for causing him to lose big face, and never, ever forgave me.

But after that, I didn't have to go to any more Sichuan banquets.

Ha, ha, ha.

Go figure.

The things the Chinese ate and the way they ate, especially noodles, literally made my skin crawl. All those slurping, sucking, smacking noises turned my stomach, and watching that sticky wet pasta dripping with greasy, slimy red *hua jiao* and *la jiao* slither up their chins and into their mouths always drove me to the point of having to actually excuse myself and leave the room. My stomach would just roll at the sight or the sound or the smell of a Chinese person with a bowl of noodles.

I also thought that the way they cupped their stupid little rice bowls up to their chins and sucked that tasteless, lumpy, white grain off their chopsticks was simultaneously ridiculous, tragic and pathetic.

But the Chinese felt the same way about most foreigners, and it wasn't only *the stuff we ate* and *the way we ate* that they thought were strange—*it was our entire manner in general.* They thought all foreigners were loud, boisterous, rude, obnoxious, whining, cranky, spoiled, selfish, lazy, wasteful, stupid and decadent, and they hated it that we didn't give a shit about face. Plus we all looked alike.

So I was somewhat astounded when a Chinese VIP at a banquet I attended once (before Sidney got mad at me and I still had to go to one now and then) asked me how we could possibly enjoy our food without making any noise. Foreigners eat too quietly, he pointedly informed me, and Chinese people thought this was very rude. How could we enjoy eating without making any smacking, slurping or sucking sounds? he asked. It just didn't make sense, he said. So evidently we were loud, boisterous, rude and obnoxious whenever we weren't supposed to be, like in general, but not when were supposed to be, like when we were eating.

Go figure.

And, of course, the Chinese always thought that the foreigners were always eating the things they weren't supposed to be eating when they weren't supposed to be eating them (like moon cakes during the wrong time of year), and not eating the things they were supposed to be eating when they were supposed to be eating them (like dog meat on a certain holiday).

One time I found a couple of dinosaur eggs for sale on the black market, and I wanted one, real bad. But they were priced at ¥20,000.00 RMB a piece, or about $2,400.00 American money, which was about $2,350.00 American money out of my price range.

I was sitting in the lobby of the office one day, waiting for Justin to come back from the factory and whining about the price of a dinosaur egg to one of my two American friends in Chengdu, when Justin's inter-preter—who'd returned early to tidy up some paperwork—overheard me.

He decided to join the conversation. Stone-faced, he turned to me and said, "Gee, that's very expensive for an egg you cannot eat. But then again, you *lao wai* eat some awfully strange things sometimes." Then, having stated his position, he turned back to his work.

We *lao wai* eat strange things?

Good God, get serious.

Good God, *was* he serious?

To this day, I still don't know.

❧   ❧   ❧

And then there was the stuff that we knew the Chinese ate, but which they always claimed they didn't.

I had heard some rather disturbing rumors about what kinds of food the dirty little dive restaurant over by the American Consulate served, and Miss Li and I were having a Chinglish argument about it one day.

"Chengdu people no eat dog," Miss Li stated emphatically.

Yeah, right.

I'd walked past that dirty little dive restaurant about a thousand times, and I'd seen what I thought was going on in there and I'd also seen the cages out back.

She was lying and I knew it.

"Okay," I said.

"Okay," she said.

Actually, Chengdu people had been telling me this for over a year—it wasn't just Miss Li. But I knew better. Not only had I seen the cages out back of that dirty little dive restaurant, I'd seen the puppies in the cages at the *mai cai*, too.

But the undeniable proof-positive had actually come during a flight to Bangkok a few weeks earlier. I was thumbing through an in-flight magazine on the plane when I ran across an article—complete with photos and recipe, and written in both Chinese and English—entitled

Puppy Stew. And, as luck would have it, the restaurant featured in the article just happened to be that dirty little dive right next door to the American Consulate in Chengdu!

I was so horrified that I'd kept a copy.

I raced up the seven flights of stairs to our executive penthouse company *condomimium*, grabbed that magazine off the top of my desk, and flew back down the stairs to the lobby. I would prove to Miss Li, once and for all, that I knew the truth, and that neither she, nor anyone else, could continue to lie to me about this anymore.

I bolted through the front door of the lobby and slammed the article that would convict her on top of her desk, obliterating the latest issue of Chinese *Cosmo*.

"There!" I shrieked, triumphantly. "See? *Puppy Stew.*"

Miss Li gave me her most innocent stare as she pursed her perfectly-painted blood-red lips and sadly shook her perfectly-porcelain doll-like head. With immaculate blood-red fingertips, she gently closed the in-flight magazine I'd slammed onto her desk like it was an evil dirty thing she'd rather not touch and gingerly pushed it toward me with her answer: "Only one holiday per year, some people eat dog," she said.

Yeah, right.

Like that didn't count.

I give up.

Chapter 14
Giving Face, Saving Face and Getting *Guanxi*

Although the pursuit of corporate glory in China often meant different things to different people, mostly it meant pomp and circumstance, Giving Face, Saving Face and Getting *Guanxi*.

And *that* meant Sichuan banquets.

The Sacred Ritual of the Sichuan Banquet didn't have anything to do with food, not really. It was all about Giving Face, Saving Face and Getting *Guanxi*. It was all about money—the more exotic, the more expensive; the more bizarre, the more expensive; the more eccentric, the more expensive. The more expensive, the more pomp and circumstance, and the more pomp and circumstance, the more face. And the more face you got, the more *guanxi* you got.

The Chinese liked to call doing business in China "Socialistic Democratic Communism with a Chinese flair."

But it was capitalism, pure and simple.

And capitalism in China meant getting *guanxi*, because you can't do business in China without it.

Now, the intricate art of Giving Face, Saving Face and Getting *Guanxi* work something like this:

It begins with THE INTRODUCTION, which must be arranged by a third party, which Gives Him Face. Of course, THE INTRODUCTION can only be arranged after you have established a relationship of Giving Face and Saving Face and Getting *Guanxi* with the arranger. You must then agree to Give More Face to and Save More Face for the arranger during THE INTRODUCTION ceremony. Then you must conduct yourself properly during THE INTRODUCTION ceremony by Giving Face to and Saving Face for everybody else there, too, because if you don't, then everybody Loses Face. If you cause somebody to Lose Face, they will never, ever forgive you, they will never, ever Give You Any More Face or Save You Any More Face, and they will never, ever let you try to make amends by Giving More Face back to them, either.

Now, if someone has Given You Face or Saved Your Face, in which case you actually Gave Them Face by letting them Give You Face or Save Your Face, then they are entitled to ask you to return the favor by arranging an introduction ceremony for them. This not only Gives You Face and Saves Your Face, it Gives Them Face and Saves Them Face, too. This provides them with more opportunities to Give You More Face and Save You More Face, which in turn allows you to Give Them More Face and Save More of Their Face and on and on and on it goes. It's kind of like the legendary Chinese box.

Of course, the more people you meet, the more opportunities you have to Give More Face to and Save More Face for more people, and that means more people will have more opportunities to Give You More Face and Save More of Your Face.

Giving Face and Saving Face is one of the ways to Get *Guanxi*, although it's not the best way. Getting *Guanxi* is the key to doing business in China, and you can't get anything done without it. *Guanxi* is the art of having all the right connections with all the right people in all the right places. It's best to be born into *guanxi*, but if you're not, you will have to go out and get some, and that's really tough. Throwing elaborate banquets for all the right people in all the right places helps, doing favors for all the right people in all the right places helps, and giving gifts to all the right people in all the right places helps. Of course, all this Gives Them Face and Saves Them Face and it Gives You Face and Saves Your Face, too, all of which helps you Get Good *Guanxi*.

If none of that works, you'll just have to sneak around and go in the back door, like most of the Chinese actually do.

And don't forget the cigarettes.

Chapter 15

The Sacred Ritual of the Sichuan Banquet

"At one time or another," Justin liked to brag, "during all the years that we have lived in China, I have been served a piece of every living creature on earth, with the exception of man. And panda."

And eaten, too, I feared.

Justin, because of his position in the company as token *lao wai* and great foreign prize, attended Sichuan banquets often. I, as corporate fluff, went to a few, but after that remark I'd made in front of Sidney about the tofu with the dog meat, I never had to go to another one.

Thank God. And Buddha too.

I hated Sichuan's hot, sizzling, spicy food, but Justin loved it. His motto was: "If it ain't moving and I never had it as a pet as a child, I'll eat it!" Eventually he was forced to expand this list to include not eating creepy crawly things as well: crickets, scorpions, cockroaches, ants, potato bugs, centipedes, spiders, gnats and beetles—be they dead or alive—were not a food group and therefore didn't count, he said. On the matter of reptiles, he was split 50/50: "Some are okay, some not," he told me, "but snake and turtle bile are definitely out!"

I missed his very first Sichuan banquet, thank God, but Justin, being the loving, caring, sharing, devoted husband that he was, described it to me later in gross, explicit detail.

It was an expensive, elaborate affair held in his honor. It was hosted by the top fifteen members of his staff and designed to impress him. The assistant manager had been charged with ordering all the food. Justin estimated that it had cost around ¥25,000.00 RMB (about $3,000.00 U.S.). It was lavish.

There were probably two dozen courses, he said, and much of that was standard Chinese fare. There were the raw peanuts soaked in *hua jiao* and *la jiao* and the roasted peanuts soaked in *hua jiao* and *la jiao*. There were the Chinese pickles soaked in *hua jiao* and *la jiao* and the greasy, slimy green goo soaked in *hua jiao* and *la jiao*. Then there were the platters of raw animal organs like esophagus, intestines, kidneys and bladders swimming around in pools of their own fresh blood. There were the chickens' feet, the piranha filet, the snake meat, the turtle meat, the snake bile, the turtle bile, the slimy goat meat, the mummified rat skulls and the prawn heads skewered onto toothpicks like little pink torpedoes. And then there were the bowls of extra *hua jiao* and *la jiao* to soak everything in after it had all been scalded to death in the hot pot.

There was also some really good stuff, he said, the delicacies ordered to impress him with their good taste (both the food's and the host's). Nifty special treats like large fried ants—red or black he said he couldn't tell, since they were covered with so much *hua jiao* and *la jiao* that he really couldn't see much except for their stiff little dead bug legs sticking out all over the place.

About midway through this elaborate meal, he went on, the waitress set a whole scorpion—completely intact—down in front of him. It was a big, black, vicious-looking thing, served up on a snow-white platter with a little orange garnish off to one side.

What?

A *scorpion?*

People actually *ate* scorpion?

Dead or alive? I wondered, remembering the monkey brains scene from that old *Indiana Jones* movie, *The Temple of Doom*. Did he have to chase it around the table and spear it with his chopsticks? I asked. Did it squirm and struggle and try to get away as it headed toward his hungry mouth? Did it try to sting his nose?

Was this one of those super-dangerous Oriental eating games, like the Japanese played with the blowfish?

"Good God, you didn't eat it, did you?" I shrieked.

Eating scorpion sounded worse to me than eating chickens' feet or dog meat, but then an even more terrifying thought struck me.

"Good God," I shrieked again, "you didn't eat any monkey brains, did you?"

Justin, whose look at this point conveyed, "Don't be stupid, have you lost your own little monkey brain?" answered, "Of course not! They don't eat monkey brain in Sichuan."

Yeah, right, and they don't eat dog, either.

"In Sichuan," Justin continued, "they prefer to eat superior giant beetles imported from Nepal!"

What?

Didn't they eat those same awful beetles in that same old *Indiana Jones* movie right before they ate the monkey brains?

No, wait!

Don't tell me.

I really don't want to know.

But the best part, Justin said, they'd saved for last. *(Better than the scorpion? I could hardly wait to hear about that.)* The Chinese eat their soup at the end of the meal, not at the beginning like most Americans. Dessert was Seven-Dick Soup: deer dick, duck dick, bear dick, dog dick, goat dick, bull dick and sheep dick soup. Most restaurants don't use tiger dick anymore, because that's a capital offense now.

Mmmm, yummy.

The Chinese claimed that Seven-Dick Soup did a lot for their libido.

Do you suppose that's why there's so damn many of them?

Chapter 16

Gan Bei

Like I said, I hated Sichuan banquets with every fiber of my being. Besides all that disgusting, revolting garbage the Chinese had the unmitigated audacity to call food, there was always lots and lots of warm beer, *bai jiu* (white rice wine) and *mao cai* (stronger white rice wine) on the table. *Bai jiu* and *mao cai* smelled like a bad batch of moonshine, tasted worse, and gave you the most incredible three-day hangover in the universe.

The Great *Gan Bei*, a toast gone obsessive-compulsive, always accompanied all this booze. In China an empty glass is considered rude, a half-empty glass is considered rude, and a quarter-empty glass is considered rude, so somebody is always pouring more beer or more tea or more *bai jiu* or more *mao cai* into your glass, even if you've only taken just one tiny little sip.

And when it comes to liquor, the problem is that just one tiny little sip is not allowed. Only *gan bei* is allowed, which means standing up, shouting "*gan bei*" (which, loosely translated, means "cheers" or "bottoms up") and draining your glass to the very bottom every time you take a drink. Which is often, because Sichuan food is so spicy that you spend entire meals just trying to put the fire out.

But the Great *Gan Bei* was actually much more than just a simple face-giving, face-saving or potentially face-losing toast. It was a game—a perverse game played by the Chinese to see how much booze a *lao wai* could drink before keeling over and passing out dead drunk on the floor.

Fortunately, since Justin was a whole lot bigger than most of the Chinese, they always passed out first.

Gan bei.

Chapter 17
In Pursuit of Corporate Glory

Justin's pursuit of corporate glory was riddled with adversity. He was supposed to be the manager in charge of the factory, but his Chinese staff prioritized all of his orders according to their own scenarios.

If they thought something was beneath him, they wouldn't help him arrange it.

If they thought something wasn't necessary, they wouldn't help him accomplish it.

If they thought something wasn't logical—like keeping the U.S. $25,000.00 generator fueled up so that when the electricity went off production wouldn't go down—they wouldn't go out and buy the fuel ahead of time.

If they thought something was too much trouble, like looking up a telephone number or helping him make a telephone call because he couldn't read or speak their language, they wouldn't do it.

Nobody who worked for him knew how to close a door behind them, even in the supposedly sterile production areas where it was mandatory.

And the guy with keys to all the important rooms and equipment was never around when you needed him.

The work ethic and attitude of Justin's Chinese crew was also quite different from that of any group he'd ever supervised in America. Nothing ever got done between noon and 2:30 p.m. (3:00 p.m. in summer), because that was the government-declared official lunch break and siesta time throughout China. And he was always having to get on somebody's case for sleeping on the job or for sleeping with the wrong person on the job. That, at least, *was* very American.

They idolized him.

Even the people he had to fire idolized him.

And although he often said that his title should have been official corporate babysitter rather than that of an engineering manager, he'd found his corporate glory.

☯   ☯   ☯

But the pursuit of corporate glory meant different things to different people.

For weeks, Justin had watched a small, muscular Chinese laborer pull a hand-drawn, two-wheeled, flatbed trailer-cart—heavily laden—up and down the road in front of his factory. Justin said the guy did this every day, twice a day, going one way every morning and coming back the other way between noon and 2:00 p.m. every afternoon. Every morning, the cart would be fully loaded with a single, unpainted car body. Every afternoon, the cart was loaded with a different car body, this time a fully primed one.

Justin was fascinated with this scenario, and said he couldn't help but wonder what sort of society, government or company would allow such suffering and blatant public abuse of human rights to occur day after day after day.

But he also said that the man always looked happy, cheerful and care-free, and didn't really appear to be suffering at all. He would stop along the way and chat with his friends, then trot merrily down the road, dragging the fully-loaded trailer-cart along behind him like it was a simple child's toy. Sometimes he even waved at Justin.

It just didn't compute.

Finally, Justin said he couldn't stand it any longer. He just had to talk to this guy. One day, when the man trotted by the factory about noon, Justin grabbed his interpreter, and they hailed the man with the trailer-cart and invited him to lunch.

The man accepted, and the three of them sat down at a table in the noodle shop across the street from the factory where Justin was always getting dysentery until he learned to wash his chopsticks off in his beer.

The man with the trailer-cart was glowing and proud. Sharing a bowl of rice and a warm *Tsingtao* with Justin was obviously a real honor for someone in his position. Once the introductions, the *gan beis* and the Chinglish small-talk were out of the way, Justin, via his interpreter, asked the man, whose name was Xiao Luo, why he didn't get a truck or mechanize in some other way.

Justin told me later what Xiao Luo had said.

It was pure and simple Chinese logic.

After politely pointing out that he thought foreigners simply didn't understand these things, Xiao Luo explained that he was proud of the new China and his country's rapidly developing open market system. He saw himself as a great entrepreneur, and had seized a golden opportunity when it presented itself.

In the past, he said, the body shop had used another company to take the cars away to be painted, one with many big trucks. But Xiao Luo had saved up a little money, bought himself a trailer-cart, and bid for the contract. His price was less than a third of the other company's price, and he got the deal. Now, he said, he made BIG MONEY every month, even more than most translators (who were some of the best-paid workers in Chengdu). He told Justin that he'd even been able to send his son to the university, something that he couldn't have afforded to do otherwise.

Xiao Luo was very proud of himself and his own small company, and said that it had grown very big, very fast. He bragged that after just a couple of years, he had four men working for him, and that all their rice bowls were full.

As Xiao Luo finished his story, Justin said he stood up, drained his beer, and left with a smile and a parting shot: "My heart is strong and healthy. I pull my trailer-cart up and down the road nine kilometers one way each day. I don't want a truck, because truck make man weak, make man lazy."

So goes the wisdom of the Sichuanese.

Chapter 18
All Things Really Weird, Wise and Wonderful

Speaking of the wisdom of the Sichuanese, some of it was quite profound. And some of it was quite ludicrous.

Like when they said that driving around in the dark with their headlights off saved money.

Or when they said that the Chinese telephone book was very difficult to use.

Or when they said that squatty potties were cleaner than sit-downs.

Or when they said that all foreigners were rich.

Or when they said that money was countable.

Or when they said that ¥20,000.00 RMB was too much to pay for an egg you could not eat.

Or when they said that Seven-Dick Soup was good for their libido.

Or when they said that pulling a flatbed trailer-cart fully loaded with a car body eighteen kilometers a day kept them fit.

They also said that elevators made people lazy and unfit.

And that eating hot, spicy Sichuan food in summer kept you cool.

And that eating the same hot, spicy Sichuan food in winter kept you warm.

And that in summer you couldn't take enough clothes off to stay cool, but that in winter you could put more on to stay warm, and that that was why they didn't need heat.

They sure do love their air-conditioning, though.
You figure it out.

Chapter 19
The Trials and Tribulations of Travel

Like all good *lao wai*, we wanted to see as much of China as possible, just in case it got closed off to the rest of the world again or we got thrown out of the country or something.

Traveling in China was tedious at best. The travel agents were rude, the flight attendants, bus attendants and train attendants were rude, and the other travelers were rude. There's no such thing as a queue in China; whether you're boarding a bus, a train or a plane, it's a free-for-all. The guy with the meanest elbow wins.

Justin once took the train to a city inaccessible by air. The promised twelve-hour ride turned into thirty-six. He said they were the longest, most miserable thirty-six hours of his life. Justin, like most of the other imported executives we knew, didn't do squatty potties—the only kind of potty available on the train—so by the time he got to his final destination, he was in agony.

Then one winter Sidney sent him to Tian Jin, a city about three hours northeast of Beijing, for five weeks. Sidney wanted to save money, so Justin had to stay in a guesthouse on a university campus, complete with curfew and hall monitor. His room was cold, drafty, moldy and dingy and, although he had heat at night, it was turned off during the day. They only turned the hot water on three times a week between the hours of 5:00 and 7:00 p.m. He was there for nearly a month, and not once in all that time did anyone come in to change his sheets or clean his room.

The second to the last week Justin was there, I flew up to meet him and we rode the bus down to Beijing so that we could see that ancient city together.

It was early December, and it was freezing. We went to the Great Wall and nearly froze to death, we went to Tiananmen Square and nearly froze to death and we went to the Imperial Palace and nearly froze to death.

We skipped the firsthand viewing of Chairman Mao's decaying cadaver in the mausoleum on the south side of Tiananmen Square. Viewing shrinking dead bodies was not at the top of my list of fun things to do. The shining color photographs in the tourist brochure I'd picked up at our hotel were quite enough for me, thank you very much.

The Mao-mausoleum brochure morbidly proclaimed that "people of all nationalities in China look forward to visiting" and "visit with feelings of reverence." It also claimed that Chairman Mao's memorial was "the most important Mausoleum of the Country and the Party." It housed not only the remains of Mao Zedong, but also those of Zhou Enlai, Liu Shaoqi and Zhu De, all of whom rested there among paintings with "the theme of praising the revolution leaders, the Party and Socialism China."

Stately colonial columns that rather reminded me of the Jefferson Memorial surrounded the exterior. The picture of Mao lying in state in his fine glass cage in "*The magnificent [sic] Hall of Last Respects*" showed a room with a shining marble floor, plush carpet, fine wood paneling and a host of uniformed Chinese guards.

Another picture showed an elaborate painting on the wall of what the caption said was the "Cinema Hall showing the documentary film 'Eternal Glory.'" The brochure proclaimed that this film "reproduces the smiling features of the veteran proletarian revolutionaries."

Jeez, I would have liked to have seen that.

Another picture showed a group of foreigners climbing the front steps of the Mausoleum. Its caption read, "Foreign friends from all over the world."

But my personal favorite was that of a group of Chinese minority people, obviously poverty-stricken, but in full traditional dress, visiting the Mao mausoleum. Its caption read, "Visit by minor race people."

These pictures, other than that last one, bloody well didn't look all that proletarian to me. In fact, the only proletarian thing about the place was the two mile long queue of people standing outside in the blustery Siberian wind, waiting for their once-in-a-lifetime two-second glimpse of what the brochure (and most of the Chinese people) always lovingly referred to as "the greatest Chinese leader of the 20th Century."

Now, *that* was very proletarian indeed.

After not seeing Mao, we went across the street to the Imperial Palace (a/k/a the Forbidden City), where his image still hangs above the main gates, intimidating all his loyal subjects from far beyond the grave decades after his death.

Outside the gates to the palace was the Chinese people's ticket window and the "foreign guests'" ticket window. That meant that our tickets would cost more than their tickets did, and that paying a higher price than the natives was a great honor and privilege and that all visitors to China should feel happy and proud to be of such service to them.

So even though this practice had been quasi-outlawed by then, we paid our over-inflated foreign guest's ticket price and entered the Forbidden City. We walked and walked and walked all around the concrete courtyards and across the concrete bridges, looking for something interesting to see, but didn't find much. Maybe we were just there out of season, but the whole place looked as if it had been ravaged by thieves. The only stuff left—the jade thrones, ornate columns and massive bronze lions—were evidently just too heavy to steal.

There were hundreds of buildings dotting the compound that made up the Forbidden City, all with enlightening names like *The Hall of Preserving Harmony, The Hall of Middle Harmony, The Hall of Great Harmony* and *The Hall of Union*, but most of them were virtually empty.

The sign outside *The Palace of Earthly Tranquility* claimed that it had been the place where the Ming Dynasty empresses had lived. "Empresses," in the plural form. But since all those emperors had been allowed to have more than one wife and a shitload of concubines, too, just how tranquil could it have been? I wondered.

The most fascinating item in the entire Imperial Palace was *The Colored Curtains of the Nuptial Bed*. They were sheer, black, and intricately embroidered with colorful, fertile designs of one hundred children playing.

Good God, I thought, maybe Chinese men shouldn't eat so much Seven-Dick Soup.

If Justin had ever taken me to a nuptial bed with curtains like that, I'd have sent him straight to the ranks of the eunuchs, posthaste.

Ha, ha, ha.

We were cold, hungry and disappointed.

So we abandoned the idea of seeing more of freezing, ancient Beijing, and went off to the Hard Rock Café for lunch instead, where I ate a veggie burger and stared in horror at the stained glass window of Elvis: the one where he looks just like Christ.

Go figure.

☯   ☯   ☯

The best trips were closer to home. We often went up Wo Long nature reserve, about three hours northwest of Chengdu, to see the giant pandas. The company Justin worked for had even adopted one, named Bao Bao, which meant that Sidney paid big bucks to the panda reserve every year to feed and house "our" panda, so whenever we went to Wo Long, we always got the red carpet treatment.

There was a quaint little brick guesthouse on the side of a hill at Wo Long where we often stayed overnight. Grass, weeds and even a few wildflowers grew up between the tiles on the roof. The blankets were thin, the beds were lumpy, the tile floors were grungy and cold and so was the shower, but the rooms at least were fairly big and had sit-down toilets. We were in the mountains, and in the mornings everything would be covered with a thin, white mist. It was beautiful, just like the Great Smoky Mountains in Tennessee. The air was crisp and clean, so unlike Chengdu. And it was quiet, also so unlike Chengdu. I told Justin that I wanted to live there, not in Chengdu. He could commute.

Yeah, right.

A clean, clear mountain stream ran alongside the road most of the way to the reserve, and sometimes on the way we'd see a farmer or a laborer or a villager transporting baskets of rocks or sand or vegetables across the river with a primitive system of ropes and pulleys.

Every couple of kilometers or so there were scary old dilapidated wooden footbridges spanning the little river. They were obviously homemade, no doubt villager-constructed, and cobbled together with scraps of semi-rotten wood, jute and who-knew-what else. More often than not, at least a half a dozen planks were missing. Whenever anyone dared to walk across one, it would sway back and forth like a swing gone mad. Watching someone walk across one of these bridges was kind of like watching a landlubber trying to get his sea legs under him on a boat from the Twilight Zone. Whenever anyone dared to ride a bicycle across one, it would bounce up and down wildly, as if it were suspended only by bungee cords. Watching someone ride a bicycle across one of these bridges was kind of like watching a crazed gymnast on a trampoline-possessed in the Twilight Zone.

Since there was nothing even remotely edible to eat at the restaurant at Wo Long's panda center, we usually packed a picnic lunch and stopped by the river to eat. We'd chill the watermelon in the cold, clear water, make sandwiches off the tailgate of the brand new just-imported-from-America Chevrolet company pickup truck and, every so often, watch some brave Chinese farmer stumble across or bounce his bicycle across one of those raggedy old bridges.

Wang loved to tease me, or test me as the case often was, and once he dared me to walk across one of those nasty old bridges.

"I will if you will," I told him in my broken Chinese.

He didn't.

I did.

Mei wan ti.

No problem.

I knew how to swim.

Thank God and Buddha too that he didn't have my bicycle in the truck.

☯   ☯   ☯

At the Wo Long reserve, before going over to visit Bao Bao—"our" panda—in the main compound, we always climbed up a little hill to a small, square concrete enclosure to see the little red pandas. According to the veterinarian-in-residence, the red panda, like the giant panda, was also an endangered species. Cute and friendly (usually), they resembled raccoons with fox-red fur. We were allowed inside their compound (usually), and once there, got to pet them, play with them and feed them bits of dried apple. And just like fuzzy little red raccoons, they would walk right up to us, reach over to us and take the food right out of our hands.

Eventually (like after about three minutes), the Chinese caretaker-of-the-red-pandas would tire of us (the panda center being a major tourist attraction, she'd no doubt seen a million *lao wais*, and since we all look alike the novelty of staring at us had no doubt worn off long ago), and shoo us away.

We'd trundle back off down the hill and across a bridge (this one made the American way, of concrete and steel), and over to the main compound to see Bao Bao. Loosely translated, his name meant "Happy Boy," and a happy boy he was. He was five months old the first time I met him, and I thought he looked just like a great big giant panda cuddly teddy bear. At that time, there were less than a thousand giant pandas left on the planet. It was truly amazing.

I held him in my arms and cried.

☯   ☯   ☯

Just before Bao Bao's second birthday, Sidney sent me up to Wo Long with Mr. Wang to be photographed with "our" giant panda in a staged wilderness exhibit for some wildlife magazine back home in the states.

Sidney was still mad at me, but since I was the only blonde available, he had little choice. Mr. Wang, along with his regular duties as my protector, bodyguard, babysitter (and spy), was also the photographer.

There was a small bamboo grove opposite Bao Bao's den, and Sidney had arranged for the photos to be shot there, where it was supposed to look like I was romping in the forest with this giant, wild creature.

I had no fear.

I love animals.

And any excuse to get out of Chengdu would do.

One that involved Bao Bao was simply icing on the cake.

Besides, just how many white women ever got to hold a living, breathing giant panda in their arms, anyway? I thought, much less go out and romp in the wilderness with one.

But at the ripe old age of nearly two, Bao Bao wasn't the great big giant panda cuddly teddy bear he'd been at five months any more. He was now an almost fully-grown, semi-wild beast, easily as tall as I was and, I estimated, he probably outweighed me by at least 150 pounds.

The day of the photo shoot arrived, and Wang drove me up to Wo Long, where the vet took me over to the bamboo grove just outside of Bao Bao's den and told me to kneel. Then he led Bao Bao—who was hooked to a chain leash—over to me, and released him. The vet instructed me to hold on to Bao Bao real tight and not let him escape, because our beloved panda, having lived in the compound since birth, would never be able to survive on his own in the wild.

The vet then retreated to the edge of the bamboo grove. I was alone in the forest, completely at the mercy of a great big giant panda cuddly teddy bear.

Cool.

I wrapped my arms around Bao Bao's neck and held on for dear life. Whether his or mine, I wasn't sure.

Bao Bao, however, had not the slightest interest in me, in being photographed, or in being free. Bao Bao was only interested in the bamboo that surrounded us, and he was most especially interested in one particularly yummy-looking stalk that just happened to be growing up behind my back and dangling seductively over the top of my head.

As I held on, Bao Bao squirmed, twisted, lay down, rolled over, stood up, and clawed at the piece of bamboo dangling in front of my face. I tried desperately to get him to sit still and look at the camera, but he just wouldn't do it.

We were both on the ground, eyeball-to-eyeball, Bao Bao sitting and me kneeling, when he decided to go for it (the bamboo, not the camera, and not me—well, not me not exactly anyway). He stretched his great-big-giant-panda-cuddly-teddy-bear paw up over the top of my head, shifted his weight, and pinned me to the ground.

Now I had a great big giant panda cuddly teddy bear sitting on my lap.

Cool.

Except for the fact that I was now actually pinned under a fuzzy, giant prehistoric creature on a mission.

Every time Bao Bao got a hold of the piece of bamboo hanging over my head, it would slip from his grasp and ricochet backwards. The he would grab for it again and it would slip again. In the meantime, I was trying to push him off me and hold onto him all at the same time.

As the most delectable piece of bamboo on the planet remained elusive, Bao Bao finally decided to abandon Plan A—going over the top of my head—for Plan B—going around me. He lowered his great big fuzzy black and white arms, wrapped them around my rib cage, and literally smashed the breath clean out of me in a great-big-giant-panda-cuddly-teddy-bear hug.

But that didn't work either, so Bao Bao, being the very persistent little great big giant panda cuddly teddy bear that he was, returned to Plan A. He reached up over the top of my head again and got a hold of the most delectable and elusive piece of bamboo on the planet again. A triumphant smile, complete with great-big-giant-panda-cuddly-teddy-bear fangs, split across his fuzzy black and white face. I could feel his hot, stale, giant panda bamboo-breath on my cheeks.

I felt it, more than saw it, coming. By simple reflex alone, and just in time, I slammed my eyes tight shut. Bao Bao had put the death grip on that piece of bamboo and, as he pulled it down over the top of my head and across the right side of my face, he scratched me with a claw. He missed my eye, thank God, but cut my upper lip.

I remember thinking that the only difference between wrestling around on the floor with Toto and rolling around in the jungle with Bao Bao was that Toto was smaller.

And I was laughing my fool head off.

But the terror of ending up with a dead *lao wai* on his hands evidently finally overcame the terror of rescuing the live *lao wai* from the great big giant panda cuddly teddy bear because the vet, who had been screaming madly away at me in unintelligible Chinese (even though he spoke pretty good English) during this entire foray, finally came to my rescue. He crept up behind Bao Bao, surprise-hooked him back to his chain, and led my panda away.

And where was Mr. Wang, my protector, bodyguard, babysitter (and spy), all this time?

Wildly snapping pictures, of course.

As Bao Bao lumbered back into his den behind the vet, he barked.

I swear, he barked. Honest.

Giant pandas bark. I never knew that.

I swear, he sounded just like Toto.

And, like I said before, he kind of acted like him, too.

Chapter 20

So This is (Communist?) Christmas

Santa Claus was dead. Justin and I were not able to go home for Christmas. A dark and gloomy boring holiday season loomed before us. All of our foreign friends were going home for the holidays and we, bitter with envy, were lonely and depressed. It was the end of our first year, and our second Christmas, stuck in China.

The cold, gray, humid air of Chengdu's typically bleak winter dampened our spirits and chilled our bones to the very marrow. Since residential heat was supposedly illegal south of the Yellow River, and since Chengdu fell into that category we, along with everybody else we knew (both the locals and the *lao wais*), ran at least two electric space heaters around the clock in a futile attempt to heat our homes. If we also wore five layers of heavy clothing and stayed close to the space heaters, it was a system that worked relatively well, when the power stayed on, which wasn't very often.

Four or five times a week, every week, November through April, the power went off at about 8:30 in the morning and came back on at around 7:00 o'clock in the evening. November through April. Every week. Without fail.

And on Christmas Eve day, every year for four consecutive years (and, according to one of my two American friends in Chengdu who'd been there a year longer than us, the year before we arrived as well), between noon and 5:00 p.m., the electricity disappeared. And every year on

December 26th between 10:00 a.m. and 2:00 p.m., the electricity reappeared. Every Christmas. Every year. Without fail.

Don't try to tell me that was not a political statement.

But the only thing Justin and I had to look forward to that second Christmas was the prospect of yet another revolting Christmas Eve dinner, like the one we'd eaten the previous holiday, at what was then Chengdu's only (and self-proclaimed) five star international hotel's quasi-Western restaurant. Justin said his steak the year before had tasted like ninety-year-old water buffalo. Our French fries were served soggy, cold and without salt. My pasta was served sticky, cold and without butter, sauce or salt. When I asked our nervous young waiter—whose English language skills were limited to those words he had badly memorized from the restaurant's badly written bilingual menu—to bring us butter and salt, he vanished into the kitchen, only to return ten minutes later with a trembling, apologetic *mei you*.

The crowning Yuletide joy of that evening had occurred when our ignorant young servant unwittingly insulted a group of European tourists seated two tables away by delivering a bottle of ketchup to their table with their French fries.

"*We* are *not* Americans!" bellowed one of the larger men at the table. "Take this disgusting red stuff away!" He spit the words out with a venomous hatred that would have made any self-respecting Communist Party leader proud. He was so angry that I feared he would smash the ketchup bottle over the cowering waiter's head, but instead he just picked it up and threw it at him. Clutching the offending condiment to his chest, the terrified young waiter fled, not to be seen again for the duration of the evening. Justin was furious, and it was all I could do to keep my enraged husband from wrenching the terrible tourist out of his chair and pounding him into holiday mincemeat pie under the restaurant's tacky plastic version of a Yankee Christmas tree.

In a desperate effort to drum up some personal holiday spirit rather than wallow in seasonal self-pity, we decided to throw an American-style Christmas party for our Chinese friends. We invited every Chinese person we knew, most of whom had never celebrated Christmas before, at least not the *lao wai* way.

A lopsided seven-foot pine tree with a six-inch trunk that was potted in a huge ceramic pot filled with about 200 pounds of dirt and took Justin three days to find took up residence in our living room the day after Thanksgiving. He hired four Chinese peasants off the street and paid them big bucks—¥10.00 RMB a piece—to lug the monstrosity up the seven flights of stairs to our executive penthouse company *condomimium.*

As Tequila explored the new forest in my living room and Toto lifted his leg and tried to territorialize it through his diaper, my husband stood in the middle of the room with a self-satisfied grin on his face and proudly professed that now all I had to do was decorate the damn thing.

Yeah, right.

I scavenged every shop, street market and back alley in Chengdu for Christmas decorations, to no avail. The pickin's was mighty thin, as they would say back home in Nebraska.

I did, however, run across some really interesting Christmas cards, and my students even gave me a card that had obviously been quite meticulously selected. Each of them had signed it, and one of them had written "MERRY CHRISTMAS MISS DAISY" on the inside. The cover danced with a delicate patchwork of pretty little pink flowers and red hearts and read: "Happy Valentine's Day." But it was the thought that counted, and it gave me another brilliant idea for another great lesson plan.

Sidney got a Christmas card from the management staff of the rich people's compound, which, printed in all caps, read:

"YOUR CARE MEANS THE MOST PRECIOUS MEASURE TO US.
ORCHARD VILLAS,
YOUR FOREVER FRIEND."

But my personal favorite, which pictured a very Western-looking Santa Claus standing next to his sleigh, read exactly:

"Let 'fhe' [*sic*] birds singing for you freely.
Affectionated your heart with friendship.
Decorated your dreams with fresh flowers.
Merry christmas [*sic*] to you."

By the time our third and fourth Christmases had rolled around, Chengdu's holiday shopping had improved, but, that second Christmas in China, I couldn't even steal so much as a plastic, blow up Santa Claus.

Many of our American friends, however, unlike me, had had the foresight to bring along all sorts of crafty little goodies when they'd made their overseas moves to China. I begged, borrowed and stole everything I could get my grubby little hands on. I made our friends feel guilty about abandoning us for the holidays, and then raided their homes like a frenzied Red Guard. I ripped their Christmas cards from back home from their walls and cut out all the pretty little Yuletide pictures, then fastened them onto our Christmas tree with bits of confiscated ribbon and yarn.

I badgered and wheedled and whined and cajoled until most of the people we knew refused to take my telephone calls or answer their doorbells if they suspected I might be ringing. I plied the few remaining unsuspecting victims with excessive amounts of free canned beer, collected all the aluminum pop-top tabs, and then coerced my comfortably numb visitors into helping me fashion brilliant silver chains.

One exasperated woman finally surrendered to my whining and pouting, as I stood forlorn on her doorstep, by throwing her arms high into the air in frustration and barking, "All right, already! Take it, take the blasted thing, it's yours! I hope I never see *it* or *you* again!" She shoved a handful of glue sticks and her imported American hot melt glue gun at me, violently ejected me from her stoop, and slammed her front door in my face.

Day after day I lugged my contraband home. Buttons and bows, sequins and glitter, ribbon, yarn, potpourri, tiny bamboo baskets and dried grass brooms, sticks and stones and herbs and pine cones, a chicken-feather feather duster, cheap, gaudy Oriental costume jewelry and bottles of sparkly nail polish turned my dining room table and the major portion of the surrounding area into my own special brand of Christmas chaos. Our housekeeper (a/k/a Chinese Mama), Sha Yi, was horrified, but eventually had to relinquish control over the unglorified jumble when I took to cutting long pieces of tinfoil into tinsel and Tequila took to knocking them off the tree and scattering them across the floor.

Party Day dawned wet and gloomy, a week before the official Christmas holiday. Our tree sparkled with hundreds of miniature lights and dozens of homemade ornaments. We prayed that the power stayed on.

Once the doorbell started to ring, it didn't stop for hours. Some of our guests may not have adhered to the Western religious beliefs of the event, but all of our visitors that day obviously appreciated its significance to us. Gracious, serene Chinese friends with their families in tow arrived, bearing gifts we'd asked them not to bring. They entered our home with solemn wishes of *Sheng Dan Kwai Le* (Merry Christmas) and bows of deep respect, clearly honored at the invitation to share our sacred holiday with us.

Sha Yi had been ordered by Justin to enjoy herself that day, and forbidden from working during the party. She spent the afternoon entertaining our ninety-odd Christmas visitors with tales of how I had trashed not my, but *her,* clean house and practically driven her insane for weeks with my frantic cutting, pasting and painting. She described the mysterious magical properties of my magnificent gluing machine as she delicately held up a finished homemade ornament and demonstrated the effects that glittery nail polish, silver sequins, dangling chicken feathers and bits of shredded cotton snow had upon a plain old pine cone and a stick. When a skeptical guest dared to doubt her, she produced the now nearly-naked feather duster she had rescued from the trash as indisputable evidence that her preposterous stories about the crazy Miss Daisy's pre-holiday antics were absolutely, positively true.

The Christmas Angels from Heaven blessed us with continual electrical activity throughout most of the afternoon, but as evening drew near I decided not to take any chances. I circled the room and lit candles just in case. It was a good thing too, because the power finally did go off.

After I'd lit the last candle, but before the power went off, Justin pulled me into the kitchen. "I want to give an ornament to each of the children here," he murmured. "Like a little Christmas present. But I wanted to ask you first, because you did all that fancy work and made them all and you worked so hard on them and everything—." He shrugged. "Whaddaya think?"

I loved it.

"I think it's brilliant!" I exclaimed. "Give 'em all away. That's a great idea!" Then I stopped and evaluated this seriously for a moment, and shook my head. "But it's not gonna stop at just the children, you know," I told him.

"Sure it will," he said with a confident nod.

"No it won't," I said with a confident shake.

He was wrong.

I was right.

They stripped our tree in fifteen minutes flat.

Only the tiny twinkling lights, the dog chews and the cat toys remained.

As I watched each glowing Oriental face, the monumental nature of the occasion as it must have been seen through the eyes of our Chinese friends slowly dawned on me. Everyone, young and old and in between, carefully approached our tree and selected their own special ornament, gingerly removed it from a branch, then thanked us profusely and turned aside to give the next person a chance. In my heart I truly felt as if Justin and I had found a way to share the true spirit of Christmas with this supposedly unfeeling, atheistic, alien culture, without preaching or sermonizing or judging or lecturing.

It was the biggest warm fuzzy of my life.

A couple of weeks later, I was describing the event to a group of foreign women at an AmCham luncheon, when one of the more elite upper-class expats spoke up. "If anyone," she said, looking down her proboscis beak, "Chinese or otherwise, had so much as looked at my Christmas tree cross-eyed, I would have strangled them on the spot."

Well, I certainly couldn't imagine why. I'd seen her tree—it was a little two-foot-tall imported job with wee plastic balls and store-bought paper garland from back home, but I, as usual, was in the minority. And of course all the other women in attendance resoundingly supported her decision and openly declared me a raving lunatic. Again.

But I was proud to be that lunatic, if that's what it took, because I always thought that Christmas was supposed to be about giving.

Perhaps their Santa Claus was dead.

But my Santa Claus…?

Well, my Santa Claus was not dead after all.

Chapter 21

There's No Place Like Home-Sweet-Chinese-Home

Everything had come full circle. After nearly four years in China, it was finally time to leave.

I wouldn't be disguised as a highly respected American English teacher anymore.

Justin would have no place to pursue corporate glory.

I would have to give up my elite status as Number One Expatriate Social Outcast.

Good God, no more *mai cai*!

And, thank God, no more squatty potties!

So when my husband Justin asked me if I wanted to go, I thought he was crazy.

I still hadn't made it to Tibet.

But only three short weeks after Justin first asked me if I was ready to leave, we left.

For a year.

And then we went back.

For another two years.

There were times when I hated it and times when I loved it.

But they actually let me back in.

Brave, indeed.

Chapter 22
Now,...

where the hell is my glue gun?

Glossary

Mandarin Chinese, *a/k/a Putonghua*, is the official language of mainland China. *Pinyin*, the English form of Chinese, was developed in an attempt to make the Chinese language more understandable to the Western world. Pinyin uses the English alphabet to spell and pronounce Chinese characters, or "words."

Grammatically speaking, English and Chinese are very different languages. There is no rule requiring verbs, nouns, and adjectives to agree with one another. There is no such thing as the singular or plural form of a word, or verb tense. To indicate plurality, a word is sometimes used twice, or a number word is added to the sentence. Words that help indicate time, such as "before" or "after," are usually placed at the beginning or end of a sentence to clarify past and future tenses. In *Ni Howdy!*, I have taken some American-style liberties with some of the Chinese, as in *"lao wai,"* and added *s, ed* or *ing* to indicate plurality or tense, as in *"lao wais."*

Translations used in this text are not always literal, and pronunciation does not necessarily conform to that of standard pinyin. Instead, I have used the common meaning and pronunciation based on my experiences in China in general, and Chengdu dialect in particular. Truly, there really is no one pure and proper way to spell, pronounce or translate the Chinese language.

Pinyin	English Pronunciation	Meaning
Bai jiu	Bye joe	Strong rice wine
Bu hao	Boo how	No good
Bu xin	Boo sheen	No way
Bu	Boo	No
Bu zhi dao	Boo zuh dow	I don't know
Deng yi xia	Dun e shaw	Just a minute
Guanxi	Gwan·she	An intricate Oriental network that deals with relationships
Gan bei	Gan bay	A toast or drinking game
Guo lai	Go lie	Come here
Hao	How	Good
Hua jiao	Whaw jow	Spicy red spice
Hao zhi	How zuh	Rat
Kwai	Kwhy	Chinese money
Kwai zhi	Kwhy zuh	Chopsticks
Jiao	Jow	Small Chinese money
Jin	Jean	Unit of measurement (Half a kilo)
La jiao	La jow	Spicy red spice

Lao wai	Lao Y ("*lao*," rhymes w/"cow")	Foreigner (White foreigner)
Mai cai	My tie	Wet-market
Mao cai	Mao tie	Stronger rice wine
Mei wan ti	May wahn tee	No problem
Mei you	May yo (as in yo-yo)	No have
Min tian	Mean tee·an	Tomorrow
Ni hao	Knee how	Hello
Ni hao, ma?	Knee how, ma?	Hello, how are you?
Nin hao	Kneen how	Hello with high regard or respect
Renminbi (¥)	Wren·men·bee	Chinese money
Ren Min Nan Lu	Wren Men Nan Lou	The People's Road
Sheng Dan Kwai Le	Shun Dan Kwhy La	Merry Christmas
Summa di fan, WC?	Some·uh dee fawn, WC?	Where's the bathroom?
Ting bu dong	Ting boo dong	Don't understand
Yuan	You·ahn	Chinese money

978-0-595-34236-5
0-595-34236-1

www.ingramcontent.com/pod-product-compliance
Lightning Source LLC
Chambersburg PA
CBHW061306280526
45784CB00002B/910